The Promise of Fatima

One Hundred Years of History, Mystery and Faith

Paul F. Caranci

SR
Stillwater
River

The Promise of Fatima: One Hundred Years of History, Mystery and Faith

Visit our website at **www.StillwaterPress.com** for more information.

First Stillwater River Publications Edition

ISBN-10: 1-946-30024-1
ISBN-13: 978-1-946-30024-9

1 2 3 4 5 6 7 8 9 10
Written by Paul F. Caranci
Cover design by Dawn M. Porter
Published by Stillwater River Publications, Glocester, RI, USA.

Publisher's Cataloging-In-Publication Data
(Prepared by The Donohue Group, Inc.)

Names: Caranci, Paul F.
Title: The promise of Fatima : one hundred years of history,
      mystery and faith / Paul F. Caranci.
Description: First Stillwater River Publications edition. | Glo-
      cester, RI, USA : Stillwater River, [2017]
Identifiers: ISBN 978-1-946300-24-9 | ISBN 1-946300-24-1
Subjects: LCSH: Fatima, Our Lady of--History. | Mary, Blessed
      Virgin, Saint--Apparitions and miracles--Portugal--Fát-
      ima--History. | Fatima, Our Lady of--Political aspects.
      | Catholic Church--History--20th century.
Classification: LCC BT660.F3 C37 2017 | DDC 232.91/7/0946945--
      dc23

The views and opinions expressed in this book are solely those of the author and do not necessarily reflect the views and opinions of the publisher.

Table of Contents

Acknowledgements

Researching and writing books can have a transformative effect on the author and my work on this one has created in me a burning desire to not only continue to follow the precepts of Jesus, but to live the message of his Blessed Mother to the children of Fatima as well. My prayer is that this experience will create in me a new devotion to the Immaculate Hearts of Jesus and Mary, the will to sacrifice for the conversion of sinners, the stamina to pray the Rosary daily for world peace and the grace to make the First Saturday devotions as prescribed by The Lady of The Rosary one hundred years ago.

My thanks to the Very Reverend Robert Webster, Pastor of Blessed Sacrament Church in Clermont, Florida for his contribution to, and support of, this project.

Above all, my continued love and gratitude to my wife Margie for once again serving as my proofreader and sounding board. I know it can be an awful burden to read unfinished works of history, Margie, and I love you for taking the time to read and correct these drafts.

Dedication

This book is dedicated to the Lord and Savior Jesus Christ and His Blessed Mother, Our Lady of Fatima, for the unwavering love and protection provided me throughout my entire life, even during those times when it may have seemed to me that I walked alone;

To my parents Frank and Anna Caranci who instilled in me from an early age the faith that has sustained me all these years; and,

To Margie and our entire family, specifically our children Heather Anne and Matthew James, and our grandchildren Matthew Jr., Jacob, Vincent and Casey who make all the wonderful things that life offers so much more enjoyable.

Foreword

The world was a very different place one hundred years ago. On May 13, 1917, the first "Great War" was at its most harsh with no end in sight. Even at its conclusion it was not necessarily an end for in just two decades another "Great War" would begin. It was a time of uncertainty and fear. It was also an opportunity for people to reorder their lives.

In a small place called Fatima in Portugal, to three young shepherd children, the Blessed Mother appeared seven times bringing a message of hope and peace to the troubled of heart and to a world in the midst of turmoil.

Now known to us as Our Lady of the Rosary, and with a motherly care for the Universal Church, she implored the world to prayer, reparation from sin, and conversion. The effects of this trifold call to the individual, to the Church, and to the world could make of us a more holy people on the journey to the Kingdom!

While the "Three Secrets" have already been revealed, it is important to remember that we have learned:

1. That hell truly exists
2. That the Great War(s) would come to an end through prayer and devotion to the Lord
3. That there will be times of great trials, persecutions and martyrdoms and among them of a "bishop in white"

And, if these "secrets" be true, we also know:

1. That Heaven really exists!
2. That our prayers can and do have a great effect on the lives of others and can bring about worldly peace
3. And that we have a faith that enables us to endure all things in the name of the Lord Jesus!

* * *

For the message of Fatima always points our hearts and minds to the Lord Jesus, He who is the "way, the truth and the life." Our lives then are to be directed to Him who brings about peace, satisfaction from our hungers and thirsts, and healing to the world. Thus, we pray the "Fatima Prayer,"

> O, my Jesus, forgive us our sins.
> Save us from the fires of hell.
> Lead all souls to heaven
> Especially those most in need of thy mercy!

One hundred years later, on this May 13, 2017, in an uncertain world, the trusting and humble heart hears this message with renewed hope!

Very Reverend Robert Webster
Blessed Sacrament Church
Clermont, Florida

The Very Reverend Robert E. Webster, author of the Foreword, meets with Saint Pope John Paul II. The two met in Castel Gandolfo, Italy in 2001.

A Glossary of Some of the Places and People Important to the Story of Fatima

The Places:

Fatima – A civil parish in the municipality of Ourem, in the Portuguese Santarem District. The parish encompasses several villages and localities of which Fatima is the largest. Fatima is 76 miles north of Lisbon and 116 miles south of Porto. Fatima is located on the Estremenho Limestone Massif, on the flanks of the Serra de Aire, approximately 980 ft. above sea level. It is an arid landscape with rocky ground interspersed with limestone outcroppings. Fatima, Aljustrel and Cova da Iria are three of the twenty-two localities that make up the parish.

Aljustrel – The village within the township of Fatima, Portugal where the three children lived. It is a mountainous region at the center of Portugal.

Chousa Velha – The property owned by Lucia's parents where the apparition of the Angel occurred.

Cova da Iria – Land owned by Lucia's father that is located about a mile and a half northwest of Aljustrel and about ½ mile south of Fatima. This is where Our Lady appeared to the three children.

The Cabeco – The hill where the children played, prayed and sacrificed.

Loca do Cabeco – The cave on the slope of the hill known as the Cabeco. Located to the west, near Aljustrel, Loca do Cabeco, is a smaller agglomeration of rocky outcroppings where, in 1916, an angel appeared twice to the three children. These apparitions were recounted by Lucia in her memoirs in the 1930s.

Moita – A small village to the north of the Cova da Iria about 1km from the place of the apparitions. It is the village where two poor families lived whose children were fed by the three seers. (pg. 46)

Vila Nova de Ourem – The site of St. Augustine's Hospital where Jacinta was admitted from July 1 to August 31, 1919. Also the site of the Administrator's house where the children were taken after being kidnapped by the Administrator.

Valinhos – The place of the fourth apparition on August 19th, near their little hamlet.[1]

The People:

Lucia dos Santos – The oldest of the three seers. Lucia was born on March 22, 1907 and was 10 years old at the time of the first apparition on May 13, 1917. She had six brothers and sisters: Maria dos Anjos (1891-1986), Teresa de Jesus Rosa dos Santos, Manuel Rosa dos Santos (1895-1977), Glória de Jesus Rosa dos Santos (1898-1971), Carolina de Jesus Rosa dos Santos (1902-1992), and Maria Rosa (died at birth). Lucia died on February 13, 2005 at the age of 97. (Even though Lúcia's birthday is registered as March 22, 1907, her actual date of birth is March 28. In those days, it was required that parents bring their children for baptism on the eighth day after birth or face a fine, and, because March 30 was a more convenient day, the 22nd was chosen as her birthday. Lúcia later recalled that, at the time, no one attached much importance to one's birthday.)

Antonio dos Santos and **Maria Rosa Ferreira** (1869-1942) – Lucia's father and mother married on 19 November 1890. Although peasants, the Santos family was by no means poor, owning land "in the direction of

---

[1] Dos Santos, Sr. Lucia, Fatima in Lucia's Own Words. The Remembrances of Sister Lucia, 20th Edition, 2016.

Montelo, Our Lady of Ortiga, Fátima, Valinhos, Cabeço, Charneca, and Cova da Iria." (Antonio is also known as Antonio Abobora.)

Jacinta Marto – The youngest of the three seers was born on March 11, 1910 and died on February 20, 1920.

Francisco Marto – Born June 11, 1908 the sixth of seven children. Died April 4, 1919. He was 9 years old at the time of the first apparition on May 13, 1917.

Manuel Pedro Marto – Jacinta & Francisco's father and Lucia's uncle. He died in 1919. **Olimpia Marto** – Mother of Jacinta & Francisco, brother to Antonio dos Santos.

Artur de Oliveira Santos – The Administrator of the district of Vila Nova de Ourem, an anticlerical fanatic who jailed the three children. He died in 1955. Known as the Tinsmith he was a Freemason who enjoyed much power through his position and ruled his district in a tyrannical fashion, imposing restrictions on churches and religious services on his slightest whim.

Fr. Pena – The parish priest from St. Anthony's Church in Aljustrel who denied Lucia the ability to make her First Communion at the age of 6.

Fr. Francisco Cruz, S.J. – 1859-1948, Questioned the children following the apparitions. Father Francisco da Cruz, Servant of God, was born in Alcochete, Setúbal, Portugal, where now a large statue stands in his honor in Revolution Square. He studied at the University of Coimbra and was ordained in 1882. He first taught philosophy in the seminary of Santarém and directed the school for orphans in Braga, returning afterward to his own diocese, the Patriarchate of Lisbon, where he was spiritual director of the minor seminary. He himself came to Jesuits for spiritual direction most of his life, the latter and greater part of which was spent traveling the length of Portugal visiting prisons and hospitals in every city, giving alms to the poor and ministering spiritually to all. Though he desired as early as 1880 to enter the Society of Jesus, his ministry took first place. The superior general of the Jesuits obtained permission first from Pope Pius XI in 1929 to allow Cruz to take vows as a Jesuit on his death bed, against which event Cruz always carried the vow formula with him, and then from Pius XII in 1940 to take vows immediately and without the need of making a novitiate or of residing in a Jesuit community. He did pronounce his vows at the Seminário da Costa in Guimarães on December 3, 1940, the feast of St. Francis Xavier, SJ to whom he had great devotion. His cause for beatification is now being considered.

Fr. Manuel Marques Ferreira, aka Fr. Boicinha – the zealous priest who replaced Fr. Pena as the parish priest of St. Anthony's Church in Aljustrel, and preached against the evils of the custom of endless dancing."[2]

[2] Ibid

Introduction

A century ago, amidst a world of sin, crime, corruption and turmoil, three young shepherd children claimed to have seen a great Lady appear to them in a cove in the small village of Fatima. The date was May 13, 1917 and Lucia dos Santos, a child of just ten years, along with her cousins Jacinta Marto, eight, and her nine-year old brother Francisco, would see the Lady several more times in the ensuing months.

From the outset the children were ridiculed, berated and in some cases, beaten because their stories of a ghostly lady of light standing on a tree talking to three small shepherds was just too much for most to believe. Lucia was bold enough to ask the Lady for a public miracle that would force the masses to accept the children's account as truth, and then publicly exclaimed the Lady's promise to deliver a miracle for all to see. She even noted the date and time that the miraculous event would occur; October 13, 1917 at twelve o'clock Noon. The precision of the prediction would logically indicate the truthfulness of their claim, yet the next several months would bring untold pain and suffering for the children because of the venomous abhorrence from those who believe their message was self-serving fantasy.

Between May and October, the children several times repeated with consistency the facts of their visions. Over the course of those months, a time that included individual interrogations by parents, strangers, clergy, and anticlerics alike, and though being arrested and threatened with a torturous death if they did not recant their stories, the children's account never changed, nor did they ever betray the Lady's command to keep secret several revelations made known during the Apparitions. Three young, innocent peasant children preferred death to deceit and many times thought they would be shown their preference.

"On the very day, and at nearly the exact hour they had foretold, some 70,000 persons that assembled at the cove testified to the unique experience of seeing the sun dance in the sky, spin around, and then fall toward earth. Witnesses as far as 25 miles away reported seeing the same events. Such widespread testimony serves to confirm that the children actually had seen the Mother of Jesus, and that He had given to the simple souls at Cova da Iria the sign in the sky for which the Pharisees had begged Him in mock reverence, and which He had refused to grant their unbelieving and adulterous hearts."[3]

Those that had come to power in Portugal following the revolutionary events preceding the declarations of World War I, intended to destroy religion within two generations and accordingly refused to acknowledge that anything out of the ordinary had occurred on that 13th day of October 1917. Perhaps it takes the unwavering faith of the innocent hearts of children to so readily believe the unbelievable. Others, as Jesus Himself described in the parable of The Rich Man and Lazarus, "…will not be convinced even if someone rises from the dead."[4]

The visions of Our Lady were beautiful by every account. Yet, within the beauty, Our Lady allowed the children to witness some of the most horrific scenes that both this life, and the afterlife of sinners, may contain. The children were privy to visions of the eternal flames and unending torment of hell. They were also shown the chaos and bloodshed of events on earth, the interpretation of which is still a matter of worldly discord. One hundred years later, controversy abounds regarding the meaning of the various secrets told by Our Lady of the Rosary to the children of Fatima in July 1917.

Though the facts of the events described on the following pages are incontrovertible, the reader is always free to decide what to believe and how to interpret the events. As with most history, there is usually an element of subjective interpretation despite guidance from those of authority. So, sit back now and come on a virtual journey through history and faith. Open your heart and your mind and this story just might change your life forever!

---

[3] Walsh, William Thomas, Our Lady of Fatima, Image Book, Doubleday Publishing, 1954. page 150.
[4] The New Testament of the Bible, Luke 16:31

The Promise of Fatima

One Hundred Years of History, Mystery and Faith

PART I
A WORLD IN TURMOIL

May 1894 – May 1911 – Bosnia, Austria-Hungary

Sickness and death seemed constants in the young man's life. Gavrilo Princip, was the son of a postman, born one of nine children in Bosnia-Herzegovina in July of 1894. Six of his eight siblings died in infancy and Gavrilo himself was afflicted with tuberculosis.

Equal to the turmoil created by the sickness within his own house was the political climate enveloping his home nation. The 1878 Treaty of Berlin provided Austria-Hungary the mandate to occupy and administer the Ottoman Vilayet of Bosnia while allowing the Ottoman Empire to remain sovereign. It also recognized the sovereignty of the Principality of Serbia which in 1882 was transformed into a kingdom, one whose rulers maintained close relations with Austria-Hungary[5]

Serbian National Gavrilo Princip was not quite 20 years old when he fatally shot Archduke Franz Ferdinand and his wife Sophie on Sunday June 28, 1914 setting off a chain of events that would lead to World War I.

---

[5] Spartacus Educational, "Gavrilo Princip," www.spartucus-educational.com

In May of 1903, however, Serbian military officers stormed the Serbian Royal Palace capturing General Laza Petrovic, the head of the Palace Guard. It didn't take long for Petrovic to reveal the hiding place of King Alexander I Obrenovic and his Queen, Draga. Both were brutally assassinated and their bullet-ridden corpses hurled from the palace window. Petar I Karadordevic, a nationalist, was installed as the new King.

Throughout the course of the next decade, relations between Serbia and Austria-Hungary deteriorated. Between 1906 and 1913, many wars were fought including the Pig War of 1906, the Bosnian crisis of 1908-1909, and two Balkan Wars of 1912-1913. It was during the latter war that Serbia conquered Macedonia and Kosovo from the Ottoman Empire.

1914 map of Serbia

Serbian nationalists were emboldened by the military successes. In Austria-Hungary, the Serbs grew increasingly bothered under Austro-Hungary rule prompting the organization and proliferation of many Serb cultural groups and prompting the attempted assassinations of many Austro-Hungarian officials. One particular attempt carried out on June 15, 1910 against General Marijan Veresanin by Bogdan Zerajic, a 22-year old Orthodox Serb from Hezegovina, captured the attention of Gavrilo Princip and his friend Nedeljko Cabrinovic. General Varesanin was the Governor of Bosnia and Herzegovina and ruled with an iron fist. Zerajic was a mere student at the Faculty of Law at the

University of Zabreg when he fired five bullets at Varesanin and then one additional bullet into his own brain. To Princip and Cabrinovic, however, Zerajic was an inspiration.

The Resistance
May 1911 – Belgrade, Serbia

The Black Hand, or "Unification or Death" as it was sometimes known, was an organized terrorist group designed to promote the liberation of Serbs outside Serbia from Ottoman rule. Formed officially on May 9, 1911, the group's origins can be traced to the National Defense, formed in 1908 with roots predating 1901. The Serbian secret society was led by Col. Dragutin Dimitrijevic. Apis, as he was often called, was a man who had been instrumental in the coup that brought King Petar I to the throne in Serbia in 1903. Membership of the Black Hand was comprised primarily of army officers, though there were a few government officials attending. The members' ideological viewpoints ran the gambit from the idealism of its young members to the conspiratorial-mindedness of its army officers.[6]

With their main base of operations in Belgrade, the society conducted propaganda campaigns and established a network of revolutionary cells throughout Bosnia. While not so influential outside of Serbia, within it, the Black Hand dominated the army and terrorized government officials giving the secret society a great deal of influence. In fact, Black Hand members held positions of importance in both the army and government with Crown Prince Alexander alleged to have been an enthusiastic supporter. Their goal was to unite all the territories with a South Slavic majority that were not ruled by either Serbia or Mantenagro and their inspiration was drawn from similar unification efforts in Italy (1859-70) and Germany (1871). Credibility was accomplished through a blurring of the lines of distinction between themselves and a more prestigious organization known as the Narodna Odbrana.

---

[6] Shackelford, Michael, "WW I, Sarajevo, June 28, 1914." http://net.lib.byu.edu/~rdh/wwi/comment/sarajevo.html.

The Black Hand, a secret society and organized terrorist group formed in 1911 under the leadership of Col. Dragutin Dimitrijevic, was comprised of army officers and government officials who conducted propaganda campaigns and established a network of revolutionary cells throughout Bosnia.

Dimitrijevic knew well that success of the group depended on secrecy. To that end, he insisted that members knew only of the activities of their own cell. Members were required to take an oath swearing:

> *"By the Sun which shineth upon me, by the Earth which feedeth me, by God, by the blood of my forefathers, by my honor and by my life, that from this moment onward and until my death, I shall faithfully serve the task of this organization and that I shall at all times be prepared to bear for it any sacrifice. I further swear by God, by my honor and by my life, that I shall unconditionally carry into effect all its orders and commands. I further swear by my God, by my honor and by my life, that I shall keep within myself all the secrets of this organization and carry them with me into my grave. May God and my brothers*

*in this organization be my judges if at any time I should wit-
tingly fail or break this oath."*

Dimitrijevic would soon learn that there was no shortage of potential revolutionaries willing to take his oath.

May 1912 – Belgrade, Serbia

Despite his own sense of loss and his poor health, Princip had attended schools in Sarajevo and Tuzla, but, in May 1912, just two months shy of his eighteenth birthday, Princip left his home in Bosnia to study in Belgrade, the capital and largest city in Serbia. It was here that Princip aggrandized the nationalist tendencies he had begun to nurture while in Bosnia. He would later say that the would-be assassin, Bogdan Zerajic *"was my first model. When I was seventeen I passed whole nights at his grave, reflecting on our wretched condition and thinking of him. It is there that I made up my mind sooner or later to perpetrate an outrage."*[7]

Princip and other like-minded political activists hoped to one day unify the independent Kingdom of Serbia and Bosnia-Herzegovina, territories previously annexed by the Austrio-Hungarian Empire in 1908. By this time, he had come to despise the polyglot empire of Austria-Hungary. The Empire was now comprised of various ethnic groups that vociferously disagreed about fundamental principles of religion, politics and the like. Naturally the annexation angered Serbian nationalists who held strongly the belief that the territories should be part of Serbia.

Princip was caught up in the political fervor and with the Ottomans being pushed out of the Balkans, he saw an opportunity. So, while living in Serbia, he enlisted in the Black Hand. With alleged ties to the Kingdom of Serbia, this nationalist organization shared his vision for a greater Yugoslavia. The Black Hand shared Princip's disgust of Emperor Franz Joseph's proposed reforms that included plans to combine the Slavic lands within the Austro-Hungarian empire into a third crown. Such reorganization could have been a safeguard against Serb irredentism. This possibility made Franz Ferdinand, heir to

---

[7] Ibid.

the throne of Franz Joseph, a threat to those who stood in opposition to the Emperor's plans.

And so, at the rather young age of nineteen Princip was determined, troubled and in poor health, a trio of character traits that in combination can have lethal consequences. The world was about to learn just how lethal.

January 1914 – Toulouse, France

While some members of the Black Hand kept busy training in guerrilla warfare tactics, various cell leaders plotted an action that might serve to achieve their goal of a united Serbia. Muhamed Mehmedbasic was the carpenter son of an impoverished Muslim nobleman from Herzegovina. He was also a member of the Black Hand who had recently returned from Toulouse, France where he attended a meeting with Serbian Major Vojislav Tankosic, Dimitrijevic's trusted advisor. Mehmedbasic longed to revive the revolutionary spirit of Bosnia and, to that end, was eager to carry out any act of terrorism that might achieve that objective. During his meeting in Toulouse various officials were discussed as possible targets of assassination but one had been picked and Mehmedbasic received his assignment; go to Bosnia-Herzegovina and kill Bosnian Governor Oskar Potiorek.

Mehmedbasic procured his weapons, a dagger, and a bottle of poison, and boarded a train leaving France, bound for Bosnia-Herzegovina. Unbeknownst to Mehmedbasic, a wanted thief had also managed to board the train. When police boarded the train in search of the thief, Mehmedbasic's paranoia piqued and he tossed the weapons out of the train window. When he finally arrived in Bosnia, the would-be assassin had no weapons with which to carry out his attack. Almost immediately, he began the search for new implements of death thereby delaying the plot to kill Governor Potiorek.

March 26, 1914 – Mostar, Bosnia & Herzegovina

Demitrijevic had discovered that not all were pleased with the plan to kill Potiorek, so to satisfy the Serbs, Demitrijevic ordered instead, the assassination of Archduke Franz Ferdinand, an order that may not have been sanctioned by the full Executive Committee of the Black Hand. On March 26, 1914, Mehmedbasic was summoned to a meeting in Mostar where Danilo Ilic, a former Sarajevo school teacher who now worked for a newspaper, informed him that they have rescinded the order to kill Potiorek in favor of a plan to assassinate Ferdinand. Mehmedbasic was ordered to await further instructions.

Late April 1914 – Belgrade, Serbia

To carry out his new mission, Ilic recruited two Serbian youths, Vaso Cubrilovic and Cvjetko Popovic. He did so shortly after the celebration of the Orthodox Easter on April 19, 1914. At around the same time, three additional young Bosnian Serbs, Gavrilo Princip, Nedljko Cabrinovic and Trifko Grabez, all subjects of Austria-Hungary, approached Milan Ciganovic, a former guerrilla fighter known for his ability to procure weapons. Through Ciganovic, the men were put in touch with Major Tankosic with whom they reached an agreement to transport arms to Sarajevo and participate in the assassination. The three young men had already been trained in marksmanship and bomb throwing by members of the Serbian military.

Tuesday May 26, 1914 – Belgrade, Serbia

Though eager to carry out the assassination, the young men had no recourse but to wait patiently as circumstances, including the Emperor's health issues, caused delays in the delivery of the weapons. Finally, the men took delivery of the first gun when Tankosic gave the assassins one FN Model 1910 pistol. They took turns shooting some practice rounds of very expensive .380 ACP ammunition in a park near Belgrade and then waited until May 26, 1914 when the balance of the weapons arrived. Among the provisions supplied on that day by Major Tankosic were *"six hand grenades, four new Browning FN Model 1910 automatic pistols with sufficient .380 ACP ammunition, money, suicide pills, training [of Princip, Grabaz and Cabrinovic], a special map with the location of gendarmes marked, knowledge of contacts on a clandestine tunnel used to infiltrate agents and arms into Austria-Hungary, and a small card authorizing the use of that tunnel."[8]*

Thursday May 28, 1914 – Belgrade, Serbia

Armed with more weaponry than needed, and trained in its use, Princip, Grabez and Cabrinovic boarded a boat from Belgrade to Sabec via the Sava River. There they handed Serbian Border Guard, Captain Popovic, the small card provided them by Tankosic. In exchange, they received a letter addressed to Serbian Captain Prvanovic, and a form containing the names of three customs officials whose identities they could assume. That letter would entitle them to discounted train tickets to the small border town of Loznica.

Friday May 29, 1914 – Loznica, Serbia

The three assassins arrived in Loznica the following day. There the three met with Captain Prvanovic who summoned three of his revenue sergeants. As the men waited for the revenue sergeants to arrive, they argued over what Princip and Grabez said were Cabrinovic's repeated violations of operational security. The disagreement culminated with Cabrinovic handing over his weapons. Princip then instructed him to go to Zvornik and use the ID card provided by Grabez to cross the border into Tuzla where he could wait for the others. When the revenue sergeants arrived, they discussed how best to cross the border undetected.

---

[8] Ibid.

SATURDAY MAY 30 – FRIDAY JUNE 5, 1914
ISAKOVIC ISLAND

It was still the morning of May 30th when Sergeant Budivoj Grbic walked Princip and Grabez to Isakovic's Island, a small mass of land on the Drina River separating Bosnia from Serbia. Arriving the next day, the assassins and their weapons were passed on to agents of the Serbian Narodna Odbrana who transported them to the first of many safe houses. Beginning on the evening of June 1st, Princip, Grabez and the weapons were passed from one agent to another, each taking them a bit further along until June 3, 1914 when they arrived in Tuzla. Misko Jovanovic, one of the Narodna Odbrana agents, kept charge of the weapons while Princip and Grabez linked up with Cabrinovic. All the while, Naradna Odbrana agents reported their activities to the groups President who kept Serbian Caretaker Prime Minister Nikola Pasic updated.

Franz Ferdinand, heir to the throne of Franz Joseph was arguably the richest man in Austria. He was viewed by members of the Black Hand as a threat to those who stood in opposition to the Emperor's plan. His assassination sparked World War I. This photo was taken in 1914.

Cabrinovic's father happened to be a police official in Sarajevo and while in Tuzla, Cabrinovic met with a police detective that was friendly with his father. He discretely inquired and learned that Franz Ferdinand would be visiting Sarajevo on June 28. He passed that information to Princip and Grabez. They decided that would be the day of the assassination.

The three assassins arrived in Sarajevo on June 4th and all went their separate ways. Princip took advantage of the separation to visit family and check in with Ilic. On June 6th, he took up residence with Ilic's mother. Grabez visited his family in Pale and Cabrinovic moved into his father's house in Sarajevo.

While all this was happening, it was learned that Demitrijevic may have acted unilaterally in ordering the change of target from Governor Potiorek to Archduke Ferdinand. Though Demitrijevic had every reason to believe that the action would result in a war between Austria and Serbia he also believed that Russia would rush to the aid of Serbia providing the protection necessary to ensure a Serbian victory. But if there is any truth to the allegation that Prime Minister Pasic was unaware of the new assassination target, the revelation did nothing to alter the arrangement. For though he may have been unable to act in time to prevent the assassins from crossing the border into Sarajevo, once there, the trio idled for about a month before executing their plan. They did so without interference. The result of their completed mission would set off a chain of events far deadlier than any anticipated Austrio-Serbian war could possibly be.

Sunday June 14 – Thursday June 18, 1914 Tuzla, Bosnia & Herzegovina

On June 14th Ilic traveled to Tuzla to retrieve the weapons being held by Misko Jovanovic so they could be delivered to Sarajevo. Jovanovic hid them in a large box of sugar and, the next day, the two travelers boarded a train to Doboj separately. There, Jovanovic handed the box of weapons to Ilic. Later in the afternoon of June 15th, Ilic took the box and boarded a train.

To avoid police detection, he transferred to a local train outside Sarajevo and then transferred again to a tram that would take him to his mother's house. Ilic then removed the weapons from the sugar box, placed them in a suitcase, and hid the suitcase under the sofa. For reasons that are unclear at best, Ilic travelled to Brod sometime between June 16 and June 18.

SATURDAY JUNE 6 – SATURDAY JUNE 27, 1914
AUSTRIA-HUNGARY

*The Austrian Emperor Franz Joseph I planned to combine the Slavic lands
within the Austro-Hungarian empire into a third crown,
a plan drawing the ire of The Black Hand.*

Archduke Franz Ferdinand and his wife, Duchess Sophie von Chotko-vato, were making final arrangements for departure on their mission to Bosnia. There, under orders of his uncle, Emperor Franz Joseph, the Archduke was to observe the military maneuvers that were scheduled to take place in the capital city of Sarajevo.

Ferdinand, a Roman Catholic deeply in love with Sophie, looked forward to the trip as an opportunity to share the splendor of his position with his wife. Because Sophie was not born of a dynastic family, her marriage to Ferdinand, arguably the richest man in Austria, carried with it certain restrictions. Franz Joseph had consented to the marriage with the condition that no heir of the couple could ascend to the throne. Further, Sophie was barred from any share of Ferdinand's rank and splendor. She was not even allowed to sit by his side at a public event unless the Archduke was acting in a military capacity. Consequently, this trip would provide the opportunity for the couple to sit side-by-side in an open car as they traveled through Sarajevo on the fourteenth anniversary of their marriage.

Sophie, on the other hand, was less concerned about the pomp and circumstance related to the mission. Rather, according to the couple's oldest son, Duke Maximilian, Sophie was acutely aware of the political tensions that existed and feared for her husband's safety. It was for this reason that she insisted on accompanying her husband on the trip to Bosnia. Once there, the royal couple also planned to celebrate the opening of the new location of the state museum.

Duchess Sophie von Chotkovato was not born of a dynastic family and her marriage to Ferdinand was not readily accepted by Franz Joseph. Though he ultimately consented to the union, he imposed several restrictions, one of which prevented her from appearing in public with Ferdinand except when he was acting in a military capacity.

While the Archduke prepared for travel, Ilic began handing out the weapons. It was June 27th and as they sat in a café in Sarajevo, Ilic introduced Mehmedbasic to Princip saying "tomorrow [he] is to be with us." Up until this day, the identities of the assassins from Belgrade and those he had recruited locally had not known of the others involvement. Ilic, Mehmedbasic and Princip then sent a postcard to France addressed to Vladimir Gacinovic, the Black Hand Provincial Director of Bosnia-Herzegovina.

SUNDAY, JUNE 28, 2014 – 9:28 AM
SARAJEVO, BOSNIA & HERZEGOVINA

The morning sun shone brightly on this warm summer day as the train carrying the Archduke and Dutchess departed Ilidza Spa toward Sarajevo. As the train sped toward its destination, Governor Oskar Potiorek made his way to the station to meet the royal couple and their party. Six automobiles were waiting when the Archduke and his entourage arrived.

Three local police officers mistakenly climbed into the lead car with the chief officer of special security, leaving behind the special security officers who were supposed to accompany their chief. Mayor Fehim Curcic, and the Sarajevo Police Commissioner Dr. Gerde, took their positions in the first car of dignitaries.

The 1911 Graf & Stift 28/32 PS Double Phaeton
that carried Ferdinand and Sophie at the time of their assassination.

Ignoring the warnings that the Black Hand had been involved in terrorist activities, the royal couple, along with Governor Potiorek, took their seats in the back of a 1911 Graf & Stift 28/32 PS Double Phaeton. It was Serb National Day which made the atmosphere even more dangerous than it might have otherwise been. Regardless, a decision was made to leave the top rolled back on the Archduke's sports car. Lieutenant Colonel Count Franz von Harrach and the driver were seated up front.

SUNDAY JUNE 28, 1914 – 10:00 AM
SARAJEVO, BOSNIA & HERZEGOVINA

To make the job of the limited security officers on hand even more difficult, the motorcade route had been pre-announced with the first stop being a brief inspection of the military barracks scheduled for 10:00 AM. The motorcade was then scheduled to travel to the town hall via Appel Quay for a reception hosted by Sarajevo's mayor. General Michael von Appel, the local military commander, had proposed that a line of troops stand along the intended route, but the proposal was nixed for fear of offending the loyal citizenry. Instead, all matters of security were left to the sixty on-duty members of the Sarajevo Police Department.

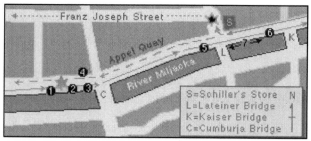

Map of the assassination route showing where each of the assassins was standing when Archduke Ferdinand's motorcade passed by. #1 marks the location of Mehmedbasic, #2 is Cabrinovic, who threw the grenade that exploded underneath the car behind the one carrying the Archduke, #3 is Cubrilovic, #4 is Popovic, #5 is Princip, who eventually murdered Archduke Ferdinand and his wife Sophie in front of Schiller's Delicatessen, and #6 marks the location of Grabez. (Image courtesy of Michael Corsini of Skepsis Multimedia.)

SUNDAY JUNE 28, 1914 – 10:08 AM
SARAJEVO, BOSNIA & HERZEGOVINA

The motorcade worked its way toward the Austro-Hungarian Bank and the Mostar Café where Mehmedbasic, the first of the assassins standing along the route, was positioned. Mehmedbasic, who concealed a bomb, stood right in front of the Café's garden, exactly where Ilic had placed him. As the motorcade passed in front of him, however, Mehmedbasic noticed that a policeman was standing right behind him. Fearing that he would get arrested before getting a chance to throw his bomb, he got cold feet and fled the scene. Standing right next to him was a second assassin, Vaso Cubrilovic. Though armed with a pistol and a bomb, he too failed to take any action later saying that he couldn't bring himself to fire upon the beautiful Sophie.

SUNDAY JUNE 28, 1914 – 10:10 AM
SARAJEVO, BOSNIA & HERZEGOVINA

Archduke Ferdinand and Duchess Sophie greet bystanders along the motorcade route on the day of their assassination.

A little further along the route, on the opposite side of the street near the central police station, stood Nedeljko Cabrinovic. From his position near the Miljacka River, this third assassin concealed a grenade. As Franz Ferdinand's car drove near, Cabrinovic threw the explosive which had a 10 second delayed fuse. The grenade, however, bounced off the folded back convertible cover and rolled into the street, exploding under the car immediately behind the Archduke's vehicle. That car carried the head of Ferdinand's military chancellery; Sophie's lady in waiting; Potiorek's chief adjutant, Lt. Colonel Eric von Merizzi; the owner of the car and his driver. The explosion disabled the vehicle, left a crater that measured one-foot in diameter and 6.5 inches in depth, and wounded between 16-20 people including von Merizzi and another occupant of the car. To prevent his capture, Cabrinovic immediately swallowed his cyanide pill and leaped into the River. Two detectives and two observers jumped in after him. The cyanide pill was apparently not of sufficient strength and failed to kill Cabrinovic, causing him instead to only vomit. To make matters worse for the would-be assassin, the hot, dry summer caused a dramatic reduction in the depth of the river water which was now just a tad over 5 inches deep. So rather than dredging his dead body from the river, police were able to retrieve Cabrinovic very much alive and take him into custody, but not before the crowd had an opportunity to exact their revenge by beating him severely.

The procession, meanwhile left the disabled vehicle and sped away in the direction of Town Hall. Franz Urban drove so fast that it was virtually impossible for remaining assassins Popovic, Princip and Grabez to fire their weapons as the motorcade sped passed each of them. Princip, thinking the assassination attempt had been foiled, began to walk home, stopping along the way in Moritz Schiller's delicatessen near the Latin Bridge, to get a sandwich and to collect his thoughts. After collecting his thoughts, Princip concluded that the royal motorcade would be passing Schiller's on its way to the National Museum. He decided, therefore, to wait on the sidewalk in front of the delicatessen hoping for one more chance to complete the mission. Princip had no way of knowing that the government officials had cancelled the events planned for the rest of the day.

SUNDAY JUNE 28, 1914 – 10:20 AM
SARAJEVO, BOSNIA & HERZEGOVINA

The remaining members of the royal party arrived at Town Hall and made their way inside. Mayor Fehim Curcic began his prepared remarks, but the visibly upset Archduke interrupted him. *"Mr. Mayor,"* the Archduke said, *"I came here on a visit and I am greeted with bombs. It is outrageous."* After being calmed down by Sophie, Ferdinand allowed the Mayor to complete his remarks. Before beginning his own prepared remarks, Ferdinand had to wait for a copy of his speech to arrive. The speech had been in the possession of an aid who was riding in the damaged car. When it arrived, it was still wet and stained with the blood of the blast victims. So, in addition to delivering segments of the prepared remarks, Ferdinand adlibbed a bit by thanking the people of Sarajevo for their support adding, *"I see in them an expression of their joy at the failure of the attempt at assassination."*[9]

While the dignitaries addressed their audience, members of the official party discussed their options. A decision had already been made to cancel the balance of the day's planned events. Now, Baron Rumerskirch, Ferdinand's chamberlain, suggested that the royal couple remain at Town Hall until armed troops could arrive. That idea was rejected by Governor Potiorek, however, because the soldiers would be arriving directly from their maneuvers and would not have on the appropriate dress uniforms typically worn for such duties. Potiorek added rhetorically, "Do you think that Sarajevo is full of assassins?"

Ferdinand and Sophie though were more concerned about the condition of those wounded in the motorcade blast and insisted on making a stop at the hospital to check on them. Potiorek agreed but thought it best for the Dutchess to remain at Town Hall. Sophie refused saying, *"As long as the Archduke shows himself in public today, I will not leave him."*[10]

SUNDAY JUNE 28, 1914 – 10:45 AM
SARAJEVO, BOSNIA & HERZEGOVINA

Archduke Ferdinand, Sophie and Potiorek all entered the rear seats of the motorcade's third car. As they departed Town Hall, Count Harrach climbed atop the left running board of that car in a protective position. Governor Potiorek had ordered the royal car to travel straight along the Appel Quay to the Sarajevo Hospital. This route (see map on page 14) would avoid the dangers that might persist in the city centre. However, with Potiorek's aid, Eric von Merizzi, in the hospital being treated for the injuries he had received in the

---

[9] Ibid.
[10] Ibid.

earlier explosion, that message was never delivered to the driver who mistakenly took a right turn onto Franz Josef Street, the original route that would have taken them to the National Museum.

The Royal couple leave town hall after making speeches following the failed assassination attempt on June 28, 1914. Fate would lead their car right into the path of another waiting assassin.

This is what the street of Sarajevo looked like on June 28, 1914 minutes before Princip assassinated the Archduke and Duchess.

SUNDAY JUNE 28, 1914 – 10:50 AM
SARAJEVO, BOSNIA & HERZEGOVINA

Potiorek yelled out to the driver to reverse direction and instead take the Quay to the hospital. The driver complied, stopping the car almost in front of Schiller's delicatessen before backing up. Princip was astounded at his good fortune as he was only three yards away. He immediately stepped forward, and pulling the FN Model 1910 pistol chambered for the .380 ACP from his coat, fired twice into the car from a distance of only 5 feet. The first bullet struck the Archduke in the neck piercing the jugular vein. The second, which Princip later maintained was intended for Governor Potiorek, hit Sophie in the abdomen. Though mortally wounded, both remained upright in their seats. Perhaps, because of their upright position, Potiorek assumed the shots had missed but because of the very attempt, instructed the driver, Franz Urban, to go directly to the Governor's mansion.

Princip, following instructions he had been given, pointed the gun at his own head. A man standing behind him saw this and seized Princip's right arm foiling the suicide attempt. Two police officers joined the struggle to subdue Princip and immediately took possession of the weapon and arrested him.

Gavrilo Princip was captured moments after assassinating Archduke Ferdinand and his wife Sophie. After his suicide attempt was foiled by a man standing behind him, he was arrested and led away by police for interrogation.

Amidst the confusion and hysteria, Urban quickly backed the car up and began the drive to the Governor's house. As the car made its way across Laieiner Bridge, *"a stream of blood shot from Franz Ferdinand's mouth."* At seeing this, Sophie yelled, *"For Heaven's sake! What happened to you?"* As she said this, she sank down in her seat. The Governor and Harrach thought she had fainted and reached back to help her up. Ferdinand, however, knew the truth – his wife was bleeding internally from the gunshot wound. Ferdinand looked toward Sophie and yelled, *"Sophie dear, Sophie dear! Don't die! Live for our children!"*[11]

The car carrying Potiorek and the wounded royal couple sped toward the Governor's residence where the royal couple might get some medical treatment.

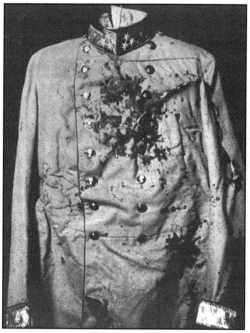

The bloodstained military uniform worn by Franz Ferdinand on June 28, 1914.

---

[11] Ibid.

SUNDAY JUNE 28, 2014 – 11:30 AM
SARAJEVO, BOSNIA & HERZEGOVINA

The car pulled up to the Governor's house within 40 minutes of the shootings, but it was too late. Dutchess Sophie had died from her fatal gunshot wound while enroute, and Archduke Ferdinand barely clung to life. He died about ten minutes later.

Archduke Franz Ferdinand was a Catholic and very much in love with Sophie. Their marriage, though ultimately accepted by Ferdinand's uncle Franz Joseph, meant that no heir of the couple could ever be in the line of succession to the throne. Though mortally wounded himself, Ferdinand looked at his blood-drenched wife yelling "Sophie dear! Sophie dear! Don't die! Live for our children!"
But Princess Sophie of Hohenberg was already dead when the car carrying the wounded couple arrived at the Governor's mansion.

THE AFTERMATH
JULY 28, 1914 – APRIL 6, 1917

As the Black Hand had hoped, the assassination of Archduke Ferdinand and his wife Sophie proved to be the last straw and brought Austro-Serbian tensions to a head. While there was no hard evidence immediately pointing to the Black Hand's involvement, the volume of circumstantial evidence was all Vienna needed to take action. Austria-Hungary took a strong stance against Serbia. Within weeks, much of Europe would line up in support of one side or the other and what was once a squabble between Austria and Serbia now threatened to evolve into a World War. No one in the Black Hand could have predicted the swift escalation of events.

The cover of the New York Times the day following the assassination of Archduke Ferdinand and his wife Duchess Sophie.

JULY 28, 1914
30 DAYS AFTER THE ASSASSINATION

Austria declares war on Serbia in retribution for the assassination of Archduke Franz Ferdinand and the Dutchess Sophie.

JULY 30, 1914
32 DAYS AFTER THE ASSASSINATION

As expected, Russia comes to the defense of its Serbian ally using its vast army to intervene. The military move starts a chain reaction of events that caused other great European powers to take note and inevitably become involved in the hostilities.

AUGUST 1, 1914
33 DAYS AFTER THE ASSASSINATION

Germany declares war on Russia for assisting its Serbian ally.

AUGUST 2, 1914
34 DAYS AFTER THE ASSASSINATION

The German Government informs the Belgian government of its demand that the German troops be given free passage across Belgium, to facilitate the efficient invasion of France as the German army moves into Paris. A treaty between Britain and Belgium, however, required the support of one against attack of the other. Therefore, the German movement through Belgium was tantamount to an attack on France.

AUGUST 3, 1914
35 DAYS AFTER THE ASSASSINATION

Germany declares war on France.

AUGUST 4, 1914
36 DAYS AFTER THE ASSASSINATION

Germany invades Belgium hoping to crush France before Russia might have a chance to mobilize in the defense of France. As the German army swept toward Paris, however, Russia mobilized more quickly than anticipated and applied pressure on the Germans from East Prussia. At the same time, Britain made a fateful decision to enter the war meaning that all nations of the British Empire which included Australia, Canada and New Zealand, were automatic participants of the war as well.

APRIL 22, 1915

German soldiers fire chlorine gas-filled shells at Allied lines causing the near-collapse of the French lines. In addition to chemical weapons, other "new implements" of war are used with deadly results. Machine guns, tanks and airplanes all contributed to a deadly, morale crushing war of attrition costing hundreds of thousands of lives to this point.

MAY 7, 1915

A German submarine fires upon and sinks the passenger liner Lusitania as it carried 1,198 people, including 128 Americans. Over the course of the next several months, Germany took many other actions that provoked the United States which, up until this time, was sending supplies to France and Britain, but had not assumed an active military role in the war.

MARCH 9, 1916

German U-Boat warfare was causing tensions between Germany and Portugal to rise, but the boiling point was reached when Germany sought to blockade the United Kingdom, at the time, the most important market for Portuguese products. Ultimately, tensions resulted in declarations of war, first by Germany against Portugal on March 9, 1916 followed very quickly by Portugal's reciprocal declaration on Germany.

FEBRUARY 25, 1917

With well over a million people already dead, a war that looked unwinnable on land turned to the sea, but the introduction of submarines and the German U-boat created the same stalemate on the waters. With neither side poised to win, the United States is provoked into the war. British intelligence provides United States President Woodrow Wilson the so-called Zimmerman Telegram, a message from German foreign secretary Arthur Zimmerman proposing that Mexico side with Germany in case of war between Germany and the United States. In return, Germany promises to return to Mexico the "lost provinces" of Texas and much of the rest of the American Southwest. Mexico declines the offer, but the outrage at this interference in the Western Hemisphere pushes American public opinion toward support of entering the war.

APRIL 2, 1917

President Wilson takes his case for war to Congress asking that Congress support the entry of the United States into World War I.

APRIL 6, 1917

The Congress of the United States authorizes a declaration of war against Germany, officially entering the US into the War as allies of Britain and France.

PART II
THE PEACE OF INNOCENCE

1910 – 1917 - Fatima, Ourem, Portugal

The tiny shepherd parish of Fatima, in the town of Ourem, Portugal seems a world apart from the site of the assassination that ignited the first World War. Nestled between the North Atlantic Ocean and Spain, the coastal nation is in fact just under 1,850 miles removed from the bustling city atmosphere of Bosnia. Despite the great distance and the vast differences between them however, Portugal and Bosnia were experiencing very similar political chaos.

For over a century, Portugal had been in steady decline due in large part to Freemasonry, which dominated both government and society. In 1910 the Portuguese Revolution deposed the ruling monarchy and established a Republic comprised primarily of high-ranking Freemasons. Amidst the political anarchy there was disorder. Despite a dizzying succession of different governments following the revolution and the strikes and street violence, the unsympathetic attitude of the Freemasons toward the Catholic faith remained a constant. Catholic Churches were targeted for pillage during the revolution, its convents attacked and its religious harassed. With the immediate passage of anti-clerical legislation, monasteries, convents and religious orders were suppressed. The religious themselves were personally expelled and their goods confiscated. Jesuits were forced to forfeit their Portuguese citizenship.

One after another new laws, meant to crush the spirit of Catholics, were passed by the government. First a divorce law, then a law on cremation, followed in rapid succession by laws on the secularization of cemeteries, the abolition of the religious oath, suppression of religious teaching in schools and the prohibition of wearing the priestly cassock.

Restraints were placed on the ringing of church bells and the times that religious services could be held. Celebrations of religious feasts were suppressed and the government gave itself the authority to name seminary professors and determine their programs. The new liberal constitution culminated with the passage of the law of Separation of Church and State, which according to the author of the law, Alfonso Costa, was meant to eliminate Catholicism from Portugal within two generations. If not for the strength of Pope Pius X who rejected all compromise with Portugal's atheistic rulers, and the fervor of the Portuguese Catholics who stood solidly behind their Pope, Costa's intention may have been realized.

The government used the disorder to *"sow irreligion in the masses,"* according to Cannon Barthas, who added, *"The times were evil. The future was even more somber."*

The Catholic resistance resulted in the government exiling many of the bishops from the country while causing the imprisonment of others. For the people of Portugal though, faith was the very air they breathed and through it all, the Church retained its faith and retained its presence despite the persecutions.

One microcosm of such faithful persistence lay on a dusty road in Aljustrel, a village comprised of a collection of whitewashed houses in the parish of Fatima. It was in this hamlet, where the word of the village priest was the final authority, that three children, related by blood, were born.

MARCH 22, 1907 – 1913

Lucia dos Santos was born on March 22, 1907 into a family that already included five other children; Maria dos Anjos and Teresa were the oldest and already grown at the time of Lucia's birth. Manuel, the only son was born next, then Gloria. Carolina was the second youngest child and was five years older than Lucia. Lucia's parents, Antonio dos Santos and Maria Rosa Ferreira also gave birth to another baby girl who died in infancy.

Born on March 22, 1907, Lucia was the youngest of six children of Antonio dos Santos and Maria Rosa Ferreira. Lucia, at ten years old, was the oldest of the three children to witness the visions of Our Lady of the Rosary.

Lucia's early childhood years were very happy; surrounded by such loving family who doted over the newest sibling to join the group. At the heart of the family was Maria Rosa, a proud and strong-willed mother who always rocked Lucia to sleep in the security of her arms to the beautiful melodic sound of her lullabies. Any squabbles that ensued were generally between other siblings all wanting to hold the baby Lucia in their arms or to play with her. Any such quarrels usually ended abruptly as Maria Rosa would scoop the child away from the unhappy children altogether and sing a song to help quiet the clan. Even when her mother was too busy to hold the baby herself, she would gently hand Lucia to Antonio who would fondle the child covering her with caresses.

Antonio labored as a small farmer and sheep grower, but he also owned several pieces of land scattered throughout the Serra da Aire. His good looks and passionate eyes betrayed his cordiality as it could be said that he was more comfortable sipping wine than working the fields.

Maria Rosa in many ways was the antithesis of her husband. She was a devout Catholic bordering on the severe. Short, stout and muscular in appearance she had somewhat of a masculine face that she may well have passed on to Lucia. She rarely had time for frivolity as her time was spent at work and teaching her Catholic ways to her children, something she started doing when the children were at a very early age.

The first thing that Lucia learned was the Hail Mary as Maria Rosa held baby Lucia in her arms while she taught the prayer to Carolina. In fact, Maria Rosa taught catechism to all her children, regardless of age, during the summer months, usually at siesta time. In the winter, the nightly lessons would take place following supper while the family gathered around the fire for warmth. Typically, the older children would roast and eat chestnuts and a sweet variety of acorns as they learned. As one can imagine in any family, especially one with so many children, Lucia had more than a few battles with her older sisters, squabbles that would generally end with Lucia crying on the floor until her mother would take her in her arms.

Maria Rosa joked that Lucia was like a parrot because she repeated everything she heard. When the infant became a toddler, her mother insisted that Maria and Teresa, the oldest of the family, take Lucia everywhere they went. The elder children were very sociable and villagers called them "the leading lights among the young people," as there was not a festival dance that they did not attend. Such dances would always be scheduled at Carnival time, or at certain religious celebrations such as St. John's Day and Christmas. In addition, the vintage and the olive picking times were always celebrated with a dance almost every day. During those celebrations, and during big parish festivals such as the feasts of the Sacred Heart of Jesus, Our Lady of the Rosary, St. Anthony, etc., a cakes raffle was immediately followed by a dance.

The dos Santos family was quite popular in the village of Fatima and the elder dos Santos children were invited to all the weddings for miles around. Maria Rosa was frequently asked to serve as the matron of honor primarily because the bride's family was sure to need her for the cooking. At these weddings, the dancing began right after the banquet and lasted until well into the next morning.

Because Lucia spent so much time in her sister's care, they took great pains to dress her up as well as they did themselves. One of her sisters was a dressmaker, so Lucia was always decked out in a regional costume more elegant than that of any other girl in the Hamlet. With a typical outfit consisting of a pleated skirt, a shiny belt, a cashmere kerchief with the corners hanging down behind, and a hat decorated with gold beads and bright colored feathers, one might think that her sisters were dressing a doll rather than a small child.

At the dances her sisters would hoist little Lucia up on top of a wooden chest or some other tall piece of furniture so that she wouldn't be trampled underfoot by the other adolescents and young adults in attendance. From that perch Lucia would sing songs to the piano or concertina, a free-reed musical instrument with bellows and buttons on the ends much like those of an accordion. Her sisters had already taught Lucia to sing and had shown her how to dance the waltz. Frequently, if there was no suitable partner to be found, they would dance with her. Consequently, despite her young age, Lucia was a good dancer and would oftentimes attract attention and applause when she performed. Some even gave her gifts but did so more as a means of pleasing Lucia's sisters.[12]

On Sunday afternoons, many young people would gather in Lucia's yard, playing and chatting with her sisters. They would stay outdoors under the shade of three large fig trees in the summer and assemble in an open porch in

---

[12] Dos Santos, Sr. Lucia, Fatima in Lucia's Own Words. The Remembrances of Sister Lucia, 20th Edition, 2016. pages 68-69.

the winter. Years later, her sister Maria would build a house on the area where the porch was located.

This is also where they would raffle the sugared almonds at Easter time, most of which would find their way into Lucia's pocket, given to her by some of the winners who hoped to gain the family's good graces. While the children played, Lucia's mother would spend the afternoon seated at the kitchen door. From that vantage point she could look out on the yard and see all that was going on. Sometimes she would read as she kept watch. Other times she chatted with Lucia's aunts or neighbors who frequently stopped by just to be in her company.

Lucia's mother was always very serious. Those that knew her understood that when she spoke, she was serious and must be obeyed without a fuss. Lucia never heard anyone disrespect her or show her any lack of consideration. Most regarded her very highly. Despite all the weddings and social affairs that she attended, Maria Rosa really enjoyed just staying home with a good book. You could usually find her reading about the lives of saints whom she considered to be so beautiful. She couldn't understand how so many others enjoyed going from house to house wasting time chatting.

During the week, there were always many neighborhood children under her care as neighbors who had to go to work in the fields would ask her to watch their children. While in her care the children played a variety of games and Maria Rosa would often delegate the responsibility of watching them to her older children.

Overall, Lucia was very happy during these first six years and felt that the world was beginning to smile on her. Her passion for dancing was taking hold and she loved her family more than all else.

Not far from the dos Santos home was that of Antonio's sister Olimpia Marto and her second husband Manuel Pedro Marto. Theirs was a rather large family as Olimpia had two children by her first husband, Jose Fernandes Rosa, and nine more with Manuel whom she married in 1897. Among those eleven children were the two youngest, Francisco, born on June 11, 1908 and Jacinta, the last of the Marto children, who arrived on March 11, 1910.[13]

---

[13] Walsh, William Thomas, Our Lady of Fatima, Image Book, Doubleday Publishing, 1954

Though Lucia was very fond of her aunt and uncle, she did her best to avoid the company of Francisco and Jacinta whom she found rather taxing, though eventually, she grew very devoted to them as they became her closest companions. Lucia's Uncle Manuel was a man of exceptional character. With his cropped moustache, a short haircut and a quiet manner, he had a look of sophistication that tended to command the respect of those in his company. Like his wife, he could neither read nor write and unlike his brother-in-law Antonio, neither gambled nor drank. Rather he was a hard worker and ardent saver who was known to occasionally splurge for his family. He was unafraid to speak to those in authority knowing that, as men, they are equals. Above all, he was the master of the Marto household.

Saint Francisco Marto, nine-years old at the time of the 2017 Apparitions poses with his seven-year old sister Saint Jacinta. The two were the youngest children of Manuel and Olimpia Marto. Olimpia and Antonio dos Santo were brother and sister.

Olimpia was a strong woman, proud of her home and its accoutrements, particularly the old, outdoor brick oven in which she baked more than the occasional loaf of bread over the years.

Francisco was a handsome boy with a demeanor very much like his father's. For a young child he displayed no fear, willing to go alone into the darkest and foggiest night. A typical boy in many respects, Francisco enjoyed handling snakes and lizards, dropping them in water to see them wiggle away.

According to Lucia, Francisco was very much unlike Jacinta, neither capricious nor vivacious. Rather, he was quiet and submissive by nature. He preferred playing the flute to dancing and few of the children enjoyed playing games with him because, Lucia said, he always lost.

Jacinta too was a beautiful child. She could always be found running and had a great love for dancing. Jacinta was also a stubborn, independent and spoiled child known to pout at the slightest annoyance.

Saint Jacinta Marto, according to Lucia, had an oversensitive temperament. For that reason, Lucia found her company to be disagreeable. The slightest quarrel among the children at play could send her into a corner to pout. To avoid this, Lucia and Francesco always let her choose the game and her partner. Despite that, Jacinta had a sweet and gentle character which made her at once, according to Lucia, lovable and attractive.

1913 – MORNING
TWO DAYS BEFORE LUCIA'S FIRST COMMUNION

Children in Portugal traditionally waited for an older age to receive their First Communion. The parish of St. Anthony's in Aljustrel, where Lucia was baptized, established the common age of ten years old for the administration of this particular sacrament.[14]
Yet, Maria Rosa had prepared her thoroughly for this day and Lucia, at the age of only six, knew her catechism well enough to test for her First Holy Communion.

With that goal in mind, Maria Rosa sent Lucia and Carolina to "catechism instructions which Fr. Pena, the parish priest, was giving to the children in preparation for this great day. She went, therefore, radiant with joy, hoping to be able to receive God in the Host for the first time. After Fr. Pena instructed the children from his chair up on a platform, he asked Lucia to sit by his side. Some of the others were not as well prepared as Lucia and when a child was unable to provide an answer to the priest's question, he would have Lucia respond as a means of shaming the child.[15]

EVENING
TWO DAYS BEFORE LUCIA'S FIRST COMMUNION

On the night before the selection of First Communicants, the Fr. Pena notified all the children that they were to go to the church the following morning to learn who would be able to receive their First Communion. Lucia was well prepared and she knew that Fr. Pena was impressed with her knowledge and skills.

---

[14] http://www.thecatholicoutpost.com/2017/05/18/first-communion-and-fatima/
[15] Dos Santos, Sr. Lucia, *Fatima in Lucia's Own Words. The Remembrances of Sister Lucia*, 20th Edition, 2016. page 69.

MORNING
THE DAY BEFORE LUCIA'S FIRST COMMUNION

As a result, when her name was called the following morning, Lucia strode confidently up to the priest who caressed her and informed her that she was to wait until she was seven before receiving the sacrament. Heartbroken, Lucia immediately burst into tears and, sobbing, laid her head on the knees of the priest. It so happened that Fr. Francisco Cruz, S.J., a Jesuit missionary from Lisboa who had been requested to assist with confessions, arrived at the church at that exact moment and asked Lucia why she was crying. Between sobs, she managed to tell the saintly priest what had happened. The tall, fifty-year old cleric led Lucia to the sacristy and performed his own examination on the catechism and the mystery of the Eucharist. After he did this, he took Lucia by the hand and brought her directly to the parish priest, saying, "Father Pena, you can let this child go to Communion. She understands what she's doing better than many of the others." Fr. Pena objected noting that Lucia was but six years of age. "Never mind! I'll take responsibility for that," Fr. Cruz said. Turning to Lucia he said, "All right then, go and tell your mother that you are making your First Communion tomorrow."[16] Lucia was ecstatic. She ran home to tell her mother, clapping her hands with delight along the way. Also overjoyed at the news, Maria Rosa immediately began to prepare Lucia for the required first confession she was about to make.

AFTERNOON
THE DAY BEFORE FIRST COMMUNION

Shortly after Noon, Maria Rosa accompanied her youngest daughter to church so she could make her First Confession, a prerequisite to receiving the sacrament of First Communion. Lucia now had a bond of sorts with the saintly Fr. Cruz and told her mother that she wanted to confess to him rather than to Fr. Pena. Without objection, they made their way to the sacristy where Fr. Cruz was stationed at a portable confessional. The two knelt in front of the high altar

---

[16] Dos Santos, Sr. Lucia, Fatima in Lucia's Own Words. The Remembrances of Sister Lucia, 20th Edition, 2016. pages 69-70.

outside the sacristy door and Maria Rosa gave Lucia her final recommendations as the two waited with some of the other mothers for Lucia's turn to come.

Upon entering the sacristy, Lucia dutifully knelt at the feet of the Lord, represented in the person of the priest. She recounted her sins and asked forgiveness. After listening to her youthful transgressions and petition, Fr. Cruz said, "My child, your soul is the temple of the Holy Spirit. Keep it always pure, so that He will be able to carry on His divine action within it." On hearing these words, Lucia felt herself filled with respect for her soul, and asked the kind confessor what she ought to do. "Kneel down there before Our Lady and ask her, with great confidence, to take care of your heart, to prepare it to receive Her Beloved Son worthily tomorrow, and to keep it for Him alone!"

Feeling transformed, Lucia stood and exited the sacristy only to find those waiting outside laughing heartily. Paying them little attention, the child made her way over to her favorite statue of Our Lady. Now within the church there are several statues of Mary, but Lucia generally prayed before the one that stood at the altar of Our Lady of the Rosary because that altar was maintained by her sisters. She went there on this special occasion as well to ask with all the ardor of her soul, to keep her poor heart for God alone. She repeated this humble prayer many times with her eyes fixed on the statue. It seemed to Lucia that the Blessed Mother smiled and, "with a loving look and kindly gesture, assured her that she would. Lucia's heart was overflowing with joy, and she could scarcely utter a single word."

As Lucia finished the recitation of her prayers, Maria Rosa quickly motioned for her to come, and as the two exited the church, Maria Rosa turned to Lucia saying, "My child, don't you know that confession is a secret matter and that it is made in a low voice? Everybody heard you! There was only one thing nobody heard; that is what you said at the end." Maria Rosa made several attempts to ascertain her daughter's final words at confession as they walked home, but Lucia would divulge not a word. Nor did she tell of her experience before the Blessed Mother.[17]

---

[17] Ibid, Pages 70-71. Also, Walsh, William Thomas, Our Lady of Fatima, Image Book, Doubleday Publishing, 1954

EVENING
THE DAY BEFORE FIRST COMMUNION

Lucia's sisters labored into the night making her a white dress and a wreath of flowers for the next day. Though needing her rest for the following day, the excitement prevented Lucia from sleeping as well, and she counted each passing minute. Frequently throughout the night she rose to ask her sisters if she could help or try on the dress. Eventually, she slept.

9:00 AM – FIRST COMMUNION DAY

Morning finally arrived in Aljustrel not unlike every other day, but things were abuzz in the dos Santos household. Lucia rose early and slipped into her white dress. In accordance with custom, her sister Maria took Lucia to the kitchen to ask the pardon of her parents, kiss their hands and ask their blessing. Following this ritualistic ceremony, Maria Rosa gave Lucia her last recommendations on what to ask of God on this special day, adding that once she received the Lord, Lucia should ask Him to make her a saint.

These words so impressed Lucia that she vowed to make them the first she would say to Jesus after receiving Him, and the dos Santos family left home for the church. Lucia's brother Manuel carried her the entire way to prevent her white dress from becoming soiled by the dust of the road. As soon as they arrived at the church, Lucia ran to kneel before the altar of Our Lady to renew her petition. She remained in prayer until her sisters came to take her to her appointed place.

The first communion class consisted of many children and as instructed they formed four lines according to size; two lines of boys and two of girls. They stretched from the back of the church to the altar rails with tiny Lucia being at the front, the position nearest the angels that guarded the step by the altar rails.

APPROXIMATELY 11:00 AM
FIRST COMMUNION DAY

As the Missa Cantata began, Lucia's heart was aflutter in expectation of the visit of the almighty God who was about to descend from Heaven to unite Himself to her poor soul. As the parish priest made his way through the rows of children to distribute the Body and Blood of the Risen Lord, Lucia was first to step forward. Her heart pounded in her chest as she offered the priest her tongue.

No sooner had he placed the small white Host on her tongue than she felt "an unalterable serenity and peace." Lucia felt herself bathed in such a supernatural atmosphere that the presence of our dear Lord became as clearly perceptible to her as if she had seen and heard Him with her bodily senses. Recalling the admonitions of both her mother and Fr. Cruz she whispered, "O Lord, make me a saint, Keep my heart always pure, for You alone." Then, from the depths of her own heart she felt Jesus very distinctly saying "The grace granted to you this day will remain living in your soul, producing fruits of eternal life." Lucia felt as though she had been transformed in God."[18]

APPROXIMATELY 1:00 PM
FIRST COMMUNION DAY

Due to the late arrival of priests travelling great distances to participate in the First Communion ceremonies, a lengthy sermon offered by Fr. Pena and the renewal of baptismal vows, it was nearly 1:00 PM before the ceremony concluded. All the children left the church with their families "separated into little groups, shouting, talking, running, some munching on pieces of bread their mothers had brought."[19] Lucia, however, remained in the church kneeling

---

[18] Dos Santos, Sr. Lucia, Fatima in Lucia's Own Words. The Remembrances of Sister Lucia, 20th Edition, 2016. page 72.
[19] Walsh, William Thomas, Our Lady of Fatima, Image Book, Doubleday Publishing, 1954. page 10

at the altar. Her mother was concerned that the child might faint for lack of food, and retrieved her to take her home.

But Lucia had been transformed! She told her mother once home that she was "filled to overflowing with the Bread of Angels" and unable to eat a thing. In fact, Lucia had momentarily lost the desire for all the worldly things, and felt at home only in some solitary place where, all alone, she "could recall the delights of my First Communion."[20] In fact, in the many days that followed, others noticed that Lucia seemed almost dazed as she went about her daily routine.

THE DAYS FOLLOWING FIRST COMMUNION

Regardless of her desire to remain alone in prayer, moments of solitude were rare for Lucia as life's routine resumed. Lucia and her sisters were entrusted with the daily care of the neighborhood children whose parents worked the fields. Maria Rosa's work as a nurse advising ill neighbors who stopped by the house or visiting the homes of those more seriously ill cast further responsibility on Lucia. Her duties required that Maria Rosa spend entire days and some nights with the sick and infirmed when the illness was prolonged or their conditions required it. This happened more than anyone liked and even Lucia's sisters were from time to time pressed into "day care" duty to give the family of the infirmed some respite.

If an inflicted woman had small children, the children were sometimes taken to Lucia's house to provide the quiet needed for the recovery of the sick person. Whenever this happened, Lucia was charged with keeping those children occupied, something she did with games or lessons in preparing the yarn for weaving. Maria and Carolina typically had several girls in the house for instructions in weaving and dressmaking. Though this was burdensome for the dos Santos family, the visitors always enjoyed the experience and would often

---

[20] Dos Santos, Sr. Lucia, *Fatima in Lucia's Own Words. The Remembrances of Sister Lucia,* 20th Edition, 2016. page 73.

recount how the days spent at Lucia's house were "the best days of their lives."[21]

On days in which Lucia's sisters were required to work in the fields, their weaving and sewing obligations were tended to at night. On a typical night, the family would enjoy a good dinner followed by prayers that were led by Antonio. Then the entire family took their "work" positions. Maria went to the loom, Antonio filled the spools, Teresa and Gloria took to their sewing and Maria Rosa began spinning. Lucia and Carolina, after tidying up in the kitchen, helped with sewing, basting, attaching buttons and so on. To ward off drowsiness, Lucia's brother Manuel would play the concertina while the rest of the family sang all kinds of songs.

Neighbors would often stop by to keep the family company while they worked and although it meant losing sleep, the gaiety would fill them with happiness and reduce their worries and fears, even if only for the moment. Many were envious of the closeness of the dos Santos family, often remarking how fortunate Maria Rosa is that God blessed her with such lovely children. At harvest time the family would reap the corn under the moonlight. Lucia, from her perch atop the corn pile, was chosen to provide a round of hugs each time a dark-colored corn cob appeared.[22]

1914

SPRING AND SUMMER

From the security of her own yard, Lucia loved to watch the splendid colors emanating from the rising sun and very much enjoyed the evenings, lying on her back by the well at the end of her plentiful back yard gazing up at the emerging stars as the sunlight faded into darkness. Her cousins, Francisco and Jacinta, sometimes joined Lucia on such evenings. Jacinta often tried to count the stars as they emerged, spying them from between the branches of the olive tree that swayed to the silent melody of a gentle summer breeze. Eventually,

---

[21] Ibid, page 74
[22] Ibid.

they were just too numerous to track however. Lucia referred to them as the lamps of angels and the moon she called the lamp of Our Lady. Naturally the sun became known as the lamp of Our Lord. That was Francisco's favorite, but Jacinta thought it too blinding and preferred the soft light of Our Lady's lamp.

FALL 1914 AND WINTER 1914-1915

The fond remembrance of these summer nights was soon replaced, however, with the "invisible poison.... of discontent" as Lucia's father Antonio began to spend more and more time with newfound friends found in some of the roadside taverns of Aljustrel. His drinking caused havoc for the entire family and, as can be imagined, had a deleterious effect on not only "his fields and his cattle, his self-respect and his old age, but also the health and good-humor of his wife and children."[23] It now became necessary for Maria Rosa to work many days and nights, sometimes overnight for many days at a time, as a domestic nurse. Mother's absence meant that the older daughters, in addition to working as a seamstress and weaver, had to assume the responsibilities for maintaining the house and, Manuel, the fields. Caroline had pastured the sheep in a variety of fields owned by the family, but now at thirteen, was forced to earn money as a weaver. And then there was little Lucia.

1915
EARLY SPRING

The robust displays of affection enjoyed by Lucia up to this point in her life would begin to weaken in the ensuing months as events beyond her control would subject her to immense suffering and hardship. Adversities far greater than any young child should have to endure.

---

[23] Walsh, William Thomas, Our Lady of Fatima, Image Book, Doubleday Publishing, 1954. page 17.

In spring 2015, when Lucia was just seven years old, Maria Rosa decided that it was time for her to take over the care of the sheep. The flock was large and the responsibility awesome for a child of seven. Lucia was essentially to become responsible for the safety and welfare of the entire flock, grazing the animals, herding them to areas of good forage and keeping a watchful eye out for plants that might be toxic to sheep. Pastures, which could be as far as a mile or two in distance, had to be continuously alternated as the sheep diminished the food source at any particular location. Weather conditions also impact the pasture chosen as the availability of a good water supply for the sheep as well as shelter from the elements for the shepherd must all be considered. In addition to these tasks, Lucia, from dawn to dusk, would need to keep a watchful eye out for predators that might try harm the sheep. In addition to some wild species, even domestic dogs might be included in the category of aggressor.

Despite her father's objections, and those of her sisters, Maria Rosa would make no exceptions for Lucia. "She's just like the rest," she said. "Carolina is already almost thirteen years old. That means she can now begin to work in the fields, or else, learn to be a weaver or a seamstress, whichever she prefers." Consequently, Maria Rosa believed that care of the flock is a responsibility that must be given to Lucia.

Lucia was enthralled with the prospect of working as a shepherdess. It made her feel grown up, like her sisters, and seemed at the time more like a new adventure than a responsibility. She had no way of knowing that the experience would alter her life forever.

Word of the "new shepherd" spread quickly throughout the village and almost all the other children offered Lucia companionship. She accepted all the offers and arranged to meet each on the slopes of the Serra the next day.

Lucia's euphoria was also Francisco's and Jacinta's heartbreak. They were losing a playmate, someone who entertained them with her stories. They in turn pleaded with their mother to be allowed to shepherd the Marto sheep as well, but at the tender ages six and four, Olimpia would not hear of it.

The following morning Lucia arrived on the serra with her flock to find a large corpus of sheep with their shepherds.[24] The mass of sheep and people

---

[24] Dos Santos, Sr. Lucia, Fatima in Lucia's Own Words. The Remembrances of Sister Lucia, 20th Edition, 2016. page 75.

made Lucia very uncomfortable. She promptly chose from the group of shepherds three companions with whom she would share a pasture. They included Teresa Matias and her sister Maria Rosa, and Maria Justino who was from Casa Velha. Without saying a word to anyone, the four girls arranged to pasture their sheep on the opposite slopes, and journeyed off in that direction.

Before long, Lucia learned that once the sheep found a suitable grazing spot, they would congregate and remain for hours, allowing the young shepherds time to play games and enjoy at least part of the long day. She also soon discovered where some of those choice grazing spots were and would direct the flock there. Along the stone walls of a long winding road leading to the intersection with the highway leading from Ourem to Leiria lay the shallow waters of the Loagoa, though Lucia called it the mud-hole or barreiro. It was a place where woman and children would come from all around to launder their clothes. It also turned out to be a most suitable water supply for the sheep. Many times, Lucia would meet her young shepherd friends there and, once the sheep were watered, would take them in a group to graze in a pasture.

The barreiro was about a mile from Aljustrel and was situated just about at the midway point between Lucia's home and a pasture called Cova da Iria that was owned by her family. That was a favorite place to pasture and play.

APRIL – OCTOBER 1915, MIDDAY

This was essentially Lucia's daily routine throughout many of the days of spring and summer until one day when Lucia's little band of shepherds set out in the direction of a hill known as the Cabeco. They took to the northern slope, climbing with their flocks almost to the top. There they were surrounded by a "wide expanse of trees – olives, oaks, pines, holm oaks, and others that stretched away down towards the level valley below."[25] The location offered beautiful panoramic views.

Around midday, the children had just finished eating their lunch while sitting on the rocks along the ridge at Cabeco and Lucia invited her companions to pray the Rosary with her. The other three children eagerly agreed and had

---

[25] Ibid, page 76.

hardly begun when, there before their eyes, they "saw a figure poised in the air above the trees; One of the other children noticed it first, this statue-like figure that looked as if it could be made of snow, rendered almost transparent by the rays of the sun." Frightened, one of her companions yelled, "What is that?" "I don't know!" a confused Lucia responded. The girls continued to pray, but their eyes remained fixed on the figure before them until they finished their prayers. Then, just as quickly as it appeared, the figure disappeared, without having uttered a sound.

As was typical of Lucia, she resolved to say nothing of the vision, but her companions told their families what had happened the very moment they reached home. The news soon spread throughout the village and one day when Lucia arrived home, her mother questioned her intensely. "Look here!" she said. "They say you've seen I don't know what, up there. What was it you saw?" "I don't know," Lucia replied as she had no explanation of what she saw. "It looked like a person wrapped up in a sheet!" the child continued. She meant to say that she couldn't discern its features, but instead added, "You couldn't make out any eyes, or hands, on it." Maria Rosa put an end to the whole matter with a dismissive hand wave of disgust, "Childish nonsense!" she said.[26]

The following year Lucia and her companions returned with their flocks to the same hilltop and the figure appeared again. As they had before, the other children reported to their parents what they had seen. Still later, the figure appeared to them a third time and as with the first two apparitions, the other children spoke openly of the incident.

After hearing from others in the village about the strange visions experienced by Lucia and her companions, Maria Rosa became quite disturbed. She called Lucia and demanded an explanation of what had taken place. "I don't know, Mother. I don't know what it is," Lucia insisted. Some of the neighborhood children began mocking Lucia. Even her sisters would ask, when Lucia seemed distant in thought, if she had seen someone wrapped in a sheet. The scorn and ridicule was foreign to Lucia who, until now, enjoyed nothing but

---

[26] Dos Santos, Sr. Lucia, Fatima in Lucia's Own Words. The Remembrances of Sister Lucia, 20th Edition, 2016. page 76, and http://www.1260.org/Mary/Apparitions_Fatima/Fatima_Apparitions_of_Angel_en.htm

caresses and positive attention from all she knew. She could not have envisioned "what the good Lord had in store for [her] in the future."[27]

1916

Around this time, having grown a bit more, and after constant pestering their mother for permission, Olimpia finally consented to Jacinta and Francesco taking care of their own flock of sheep. It's possible that Olimpia wanted to do something that might help Jacinta overcome the immense disappointment she felt at the refusal of Fr. Pena to grant her permission to make her First Communion at age six as Lucia had. Jacinta had studied hard and felt prepared for the testing. She referred to the Host as the Hidden Jesus and wanted desperately to receive him at Communion. But it was not to be, as after his examination of Jacinta, Fr. Pena's "thought the child too young and unprepared" to receive the sacrament. Jacinta grieved and her disappointment could not be disguised. Yet, it was not in her nature to brood for too long over something and the news given by Olimpia caused in Jacinta so much joy that she, with Francisco in tow, ran to Lucia's house to tell her the great news.[28]

Lucia loved her cousins and enjoyed spending some time with them at play, but the thought of being with them from dusk to dawn, seven days per week, is not a concept she particularly relished. Yet, perhaps thinking that the change of companionship would be good or maybe out of a sense of familial obligation, Lucia agreed to spend her time with Jacinta and Francisco, to the exclusion of the other young shepherds, in the pasturing of their flocks.

---

[27] Dos Santos, Sr. Lucia, Fatima in Lucia's Own Words. The Remembrances of Sister Lucia, 20th Edition, 2016. page 77.
[28] Ibid, page 37.

SPRING – APRIL OR MAY

As noted earlier most of Europe, as was much of the balance of the world, was in disarray, but in the spring of 1916, some remote and inaccessible places had not yet been too impacted. So, life in the Serra da Aire went about pretty much as it did before the start of the great war. To the peasants of such regions, the amount of rainfall and the price of wool are of far greater concern than the change of leadership in remote governments of the world. Those priorities didn't change even when Portugal officially entered World War I on March 9, 1916. Not even the government leaders in Portugal heeded Pope Benedict XV when just a few days prior he called for "all men of good will to have recourse to prayer and mortification rather than hatred," warning of the "ruin that would come to all Europe if his words were not heeded." With spring came planting time and that was a priority to the farmers of Aljustrel.[29]

For the three little shepherd children of Fatima nothing mattered except taking their sheep to pasture and enjoying the games and laughter that the late morning and afternoon would bring. Generally, after settling into a suitable pasture for the flock, the children would entertain themselves for hours playing games. Outgrowing the more childish games of "Buttons" and "Pass the Ring," the three children found greater enjoyment these days in playing cards. They routinely carried two packs, one from Lucia's house and another from the Marto abode. Games such as "Dressing the Queen" and "Sobering up the King" now occupied a greater portion of their time. They also enjoyed singing and dancing and Jacinta loved to chase butterflies and pick wild flowers.

The children would take a break from their games long enough to eat lunch, enjoy an afternoon snack and say the Rosary. As did all good Catholics, the three little shepherds would always kneel while saying the Rosary, but over time, they discovered a way to abbreviate the long prayer by reducing each individual prayer to a recitation of the title only, thus freeing up more time for afternoon games. And that's how it was as the spring turned to summer.

---

[29] Walsh, William Thomas, Our Lady of Fatima, Image Book, Doubleday Publishing, 1954. page 34.

EARLY SUMMER – JUNE

The cousins had been caring for their parent's sheep for some time now and had settled into a routine. Nothing much changed from day to day and there was generally nothing extraordinary to report from their time at pasture. That all changed on one warm, sun-drenched day of summer 1916.

The children met as usual and led their sheep just west of Aljustrel to Chousa Velha, a piece of land owned by Lucia's father on the eastern slope of Cabeco hill. The sheep grazed as the shepherds played their games.

ABOUT 10:00 AM

The powder blue morning sky was now overcast. It happened rather suddenly and without immediate notice, but soon it was raining, more of a fine, refreshing mist really. Within minutes, a cold breeze began to blow, a sure sign that a storm was moving in rather fast. The children moved swiftly up the side of the hill to the south of the valley prodding the sheep along the way. Reaching Cabeco, a rocky crest of the southern slope, they guided the sheep to the security of an olive grove while sheltering themselves in a cave cut in the nearby rocks. The "cave" was more of a large overhanging rock that offered enough space underneath to provide shelter from most rain storms or heavy winds blowing from the north or northwest. Lucia was somewhat familiar with the area because it was owned by her godfather Anastacio.

From that vantage point Lucia noticed that she could see the little village in which she was born, her parents' home, and the hamlets of Casa Velha and Eira da Pedra. An olive grove that was owned by several people extended right to the confines of the two hamlets. The three children continued to play their games, ate lunch and knelt to pray the Rosary. No sooner had they finished praying when the rain stopped as suddenly as it had begun. The breaking clouds once again exposed the hot sun and the children tossed small stones toward the valley below.

This activity gave way to another strong gust of wind that bent the tree tops as never before. The children looked up startled to see what was happening as it had been unusually calm just moments prior. As they looked skyward, they noticed a light approaching from the west. The light moved closer settling over an olive tree at the entrance of the cave. The children could discern a figure not unlike the one Lucia had seen previously while playing with her other companions. Neither six-year old Jacinta nor her eight-year old brother Francisco had seen the apparition before and Lucia hadn't ever mentioned the prior visions to them.

Lucia noticed, unlike her prior encounter, that this vision had distinguishable features about it. It was a young man, maybe fourteen or fifteen years of age. Whiter than snow in appearance the boy seemed to be transparent allowing the sun to shine right through him. And it was beautiful! Upon coming to rest in front and slightly above them the vision spoke. "Do not be afraid! I am the Angel of Peace. Pray with me." The Angel fell to his knees and bowed down until his forehead touched the ground. He asked the children to three times repeat, "My God, I believe, I adore, I hope and I love You! I ask pardon of You for those who do not believe, do not adore, do not hope and do not love you." The Angel then rose to his feet and said "Pray thus. The Hearts of Jesus and Mary are attentive to the voice of your supplications." As he said these words, the Angel left them.

During the time of the apparition, the children were in a trance-like state, almost unaware of their own existence. That state of ecstasy remained a long time as the children continued to kneel in prayer following the Angel's departure. It was Francesco who finally broke the trance noting that he had to stand as the prostrate position was hurting his back. Standing, they all felt weak and still somewhat dazed. They were still incredulous and excited as they collected their sheep and Lucia warned Francisco and Jacinta to say nothing about this vision to anyone. She was keenly aware of the end result when such things are reported to unbelieving town folk. Fortunately, her cousins complied.[30]

---

[30] Dos Santos, Sr. Lucia, Fatima in Lucia's Own Words. The Remembrances of Sister Lucia, 20th Edition, 2016, Page 77-78; also, Society of St. Pius X – http://sspx.org/en/fatima_angel_apparitions_peace, and http://www.theholy-rosary.org/fatimaapparitions; also Walsh, William Thomas, Our Lady of Fatima, Image Book, Doubleday Publishing, 1954. pages 35-36.

JUNE – JULY

As can be imagined, this event was a transformative experience for the three children and The Angel's words, Lucia noted, "engraved themselves so deeply" in their minds, that they "could never forget them." In the days and weeks that followed, the three "seers" spent long periods of time in prayer, repeating the Angel's words and mimicking his prostrate position until exhaustion overtook them.

More than once the children wondered who the Angel of Peace was and why he chose to appear to them. There are many Angels in the Catholic tradition and within their ranks there is a hierarchical structure. Catholics learn that Angels, though mentioned frequently in the Bible, tend to appear with less regularity and do frequently speak to those that see them. The Bible teaches that Tobias was guided by the Archangel Raphael, the Angel of health, joy and travelers. It was Archangel Gabriel that appeared to Mary with news that she would give birth to the Savior of the world. But only Archangel Michael is known in Catholic tradition as the Angel of Peace. Ironically, Michael is the same heavenly warrior who is credited with casting Lucifer and his followers from heaven. Could it be that it was Michael who appeared to the children of Fatima?

JULY OR AUGUST

The sweltering heat of summer remained and the children continued each day to take the sheep to pasture and to repeat the prayer of the Angel. On this particular day, one of the hottest days of the summer, the children took the sheep home to provide them some respite from the intense heat during the hours of their siesta, following which the children went to the old well at the bottom of the garden behind Lucia's home. There, in an area they called Arneiro, they could play in the shade of some fig trees.

There was no approaching light, no warning at all, but when the children looked, the Angel stood there beside them. "What are you doing?" he asked. "Pray, pray very much! The most holy Hearts of Jesus and Mary have designs of mercy on you. Offer prayers and sacrifices constantly to the Most High." The children were puzzled by this but only Lucia had the courage to ask, "How are we to make sacrifices?" "Make of everything you can a sacrifice, and offer it to God as an act of reparation for the sins by which He is offended, and in supplication for the conversion of sinners. You will thus draw down peace upon your country. I am its Angel Guardian, the Angel of Portugal. Above all, accept and bear with submission, the suffering which the Lord will send you."[31] Completing his words, the Angel vanished. As had happened a few weeks earlier, the children remained in a state of ecstasy, praying for some time after the Angel's departure.

Like the first siting, Francisco had seen the Angel, but could not hear his voice, so later that day he asked what the Angel had said. Lucia and Jacinta explained it to him. "But how can we suffer?" he asked. "We're not sick. We have enough to eat, and a place to live." Francisco would soon learn the meaning of the Angel's message when his oldest brother was called to serve in World War I. Even 7-year old Jacinta grasped the meaning. She was "depressed by the worry at home and stories of death on the battlefield, as well as the trouble that had come to Lucia's family when her father began to spend all his money in the wine shops." Stretching out her arms she would cry out, "Lord, we offer Thee all these sufferings for the conversion of poor sinners."[32]

[31] Dos Santos, Sr. Lucia, Fatima in Lucia's Own Words. The Remembrances of Sister Lucia, 20th Edition, 2016, Page 77-78; also, https://www.ewtn.com/fatima/jacinta-marto.asp; also, Walsh, William Thomas, Our Lady of Fatima, Image Book, Doubleday Publishing, 1954. pages 39-40.

[32] Walsh, William Thomas, Our Lady of Fatima, Image Book, Doubleday Publishing, 1954. pages 40-41; also, Source - Society of St. Pius X - http://sspx.org/en/fatima_angel_apparitions_peace; also, http://www.theholyrosary.org/fatimaapparitions.

LATE SEPTEMBER OR OCTOBER

Even with the passage of several more weeks, the three visionaries could not forget the angelic visions that had left such an indelible mark on them. As much as they wished they could spend the days in prayer and remembrance, they still needed to tend to their responsibilities as shepherds. So, at summer's end, the children found themselves once again pasturing the sheep on property belonging to Lucia's parents. This particular pasture was another slope of the hill called Chousa Velha a little higher up than Vilinhos in the olive grove of Pregueira.

The children finished their lunch and made their way to a hollow among the rocks on the opposite side of the hill. This area was accessible only by rounding the slope and climbing over some rocks above the Pregueira. The climb was difficult for the children, but perhaps more so for the sheep that struggled greatly to follow their little shepherds. As soon as they arrived and placed the flock in a suitable place to graze, they fell to their knees and prostrated themselves with foreheads touching the ground. They were reciting the prayer of the Angel when "an extraordinary light shone upon" them. The children jumped up to see what it was and saw, for the third time, the vision of the Angel. In his left hand, the Angel of Peace held a chalice over which was suspended a Host. From the Host beads of blood dripped into the chalice below. The Angel knelt beside the children leaving the chalice suspended in the air. As he did this he asked the children to repeat three times; *"Most Holy Trinity, Father, Son and Holy Spirit, I adore You profoundly, and I offer You the most precious Body, Blood, Soul and Divinity of Jesus Christ, present in all the tabernacles of the world, in reparation for the outrages, sacrileges and indifference with which He Himself is offended. And, through the infinite merits of His Most Sacred Heart, and the Immaculate Heart of Mary, I beg of You the conversion of poor sinners."* "Then, rising, the Angel took the chalice and the Host in his hands." He gave the Sacred Host to Lucia, and shared the Blood from the chalice between Jacinta and Francisco who had not yet received their First Communion. As the Angel put the chalice to their lips He said, *"Take and drink the Body and Blood of Jesus Christ, horribly outraged by ungrateful men! Make reparation for their crimes and console your God."*[33]

---

[33] Walsh, William Thomas, Our Lady of Fatima, Image Book, Doubleday Publishing, 1954. Pages 42-43.

The Angel once again prostrated himself as did the children. Together they repeated three more times the prayer with the Angel. The Angel departed them leaving the children in a state of ecstasy. The intensity of the experience, sensing the actual presence of God, left them weak and drained of all energy. Francisco was the first of the three to return to reality and informed the others that it was near dark. It took all their strength to gather the flock and make the trek down the hill and back home. They walked in silence for a long while until Francisco finally broke the silence noting, "I like very much to see the Angel, but the worst of it is that afterwards we can't do anything. I can't even walk. I don't know what's wrong with me."

It was a few days before the children regained their energy and felt normal again. Francisco asked Lucia, "The Angel gave you Holy Communion. But what was it that he gave me and Jacinta?" "It was Holy Communion," Jacinta said quickly before Lucia had a chance to respond. "Didn't you see that it was the Blood that fell from the Host?" "I felt that God was in me," Francisco continued. "But I didn't know how it was." Then, prostrating himself on the ground, Francisco repeated the second prayer of the Angel, and remained there in prayer for a long time. Thus, Lucia later noted that Francisco and Jacinta, though not having yet received their First Communion, regarded this as their sacramental Communion.[34]

So much had taken place in Lucia's life and in that of her cousins following the glorious day of her First Holy Communion. Life between the ages of seven and ten had been eventful for her to say the least, but little did she know that God's divine plan for her and her cousins would alter their lives and impact the faith of millions more. The visions of the Angel of Portugal and his message had separated the three children from their playmates but perhaps more importantly, it prepared them for the apparitions and the suffering to come.[35]

---

[34] Dos Santos, Sr. Lucia, Fatima in Lucia's Own Words. The Remembrances of Sister Lucia, 20th Edition, 2016, Page 79.

[35] Walsh, William Thomas, Our Lady of Fatima, Image Book, Doubleday Publishing. 1954. Also,

https://www.ewtn.com/fatima/jacinta-marto.asp. Also, Society of St. Pius X - http://sspx.org/en/fatima_angel_apparitions_peace, and http://www.theholy-rosary.org/fatimaapparitions

PART III
NOTHING WILL EVER BE THE SAME

1917

The changes in the lives of the three little shepherd children were not the only changes taking place in Fatima. Fr. Pena no longer served the Church of St. Anthony, having been replaced by Reverend Father Coicinha whose actual name was Fr. Manuel Marques Ferreira. Fr. Ferreira was most zealous and preached against the pagan custom of endless dancing, something that had been all too common in the parish.

He spoke so incessantly about the evils of the custom that Maria Rosa forbade Lucia's sisters to attend any further amusements. Some in the neighborhood questioned the wisdom of a new priest suddenly classifying dancing as the devil's work, but Maria Rosa was steadfast in her obedience to the priest and her children attended the dances no more.

Soon many other area children, following the example set by the dos Santos sisters, began to refrain from such amusements causing the custom to gradually die out. Those who loved to dance as much as Lucia and Jacinta found the prohibition unpleasant. Maria Rosa, however, did allow for some dancing in the home as Fr. Ferreira found no sin in that.[36]

There were several other changes impacting the dos Santos home too. It was also during this time that Maria and Teresa, the oldest of Lucia's sisters, married and left home. Her father Antonio fell into bad company and began to drink, causing the family to lose some of their property. His dislike for the new parish priest also caused him to leave St. Anthony's for a time and fulfil his Catholic obligations in Vila Nova de Ourem.

The loss of Antonio's productivity caused the family livelihood to diminish forcing Maria Rosa to send Lucia's other sisters, Gloria and Carolina to work as servants. The confluence of these three factors; Antonio's diminished capacity to provide, Lucia's two eldest sisters no longer living at home, and Gloria and Carolina working out of the home, caused all domestic responsibil-

---

[36] Dos Santos, Sr. Lucia, Fatima in Lucia's Own Words. The Remembrances of Sister Lucia, 20th Edition, 2016. page 80.

ities to fall to the only three that remained. Consequently, Lucia's brother Manuel was charged with caring for the few remaining fields and Lucia with pasturing the sheep while Maria Rosa took care of the house.

During this time Lucia's mother was clearly distressed. When gathered around the fire in the evening, waiting for Antonio to return for supper, Maria Rosa would stare at the empty places at the dinner table once occupied by Maria and Teresa and proclaim through her tears, "My God, where has all the joy of our home gone?" Manuel and Lucia would weep with her as Lucia was heartbroken with sorrow.

During these times, Lucia would take comfort in the Angel's words; *"Above all, accept submissively the sacrifices that the Lord will send you,"* and she would escape to a solitary place, generally at the well at the end of the garden so her mother would not be more distressed by Lucia's own sadness. There, she would fall to her knees and peer into the well as she leaned over the edge of the stone slabs that covered it. Lucia's tears fell softly into the well mingling with the waters below as she offered her suffering to God. Sometimes Francisco and Jacinta would stop by and find Lucia in distress, unable to speak because of her sobbing. Her cousins would share Lucia's grief weeping themselves until Jacinta offered out loud, "My God, it is as an act of reparation, and for the conversion of sinners, that we offer You all these sufferings and sacrifices."

It wasn't long before Maria Rosa started to experience a deterioration of her own health because of her immense distress forcing her to ask that her daughter Gloria return home to help care for her and the house. Despite consultations with surgeons and doctors and "recourse to every kind of remedy," there was no improvement in Maria Rosa's condition.

One day, Fr. Ferreira offered to take her to Leiria in his mule cart where she would be able to consult with additional doctors. Lucia's sister Teresa accompanied them on the trip, but her mother grew so weary from the number of consultations and the arduous journey, that she arrived home "half dead."

Fortunately, a surgeon from Sao Mamede, a civil parish in the municipality of Lisbon about 67 miles south of Fatima, was able to at least provide a diagnosis of what ailed Maria Rosa. He recommended treatment for a cardiac lesion, a dislocated spinal vertebra and fallen kidneys. He prescribed some medication that seemed to bring about a bit of improvement to her health granting her at least some relief.

Also during this time, Manuel became of age for enlistment in the army of Portugal. With his excellent health and the ravages of World War I in full swing, it seemed sure that he would be drafted into service. Manuel's godfather promised Maria Rosa that he would obtain an exemption because of their extraordinary family circumstances and he contacted the doctor responsible for Manuel's medical examination. Despite Manuel's godfather's good intentions, Maria Rosa feared Manuel's loss from the family and quickly sent for Carolina to return home to help look after the land. By the grace of God, however, the exemption was granted, much to the relief Maria Rosa.

SUNDAY MAY 13, 1917

Such were the events of the world and the condition of Lucia's family as Sunday, May 13, 1917 dawned. The day was bright and fair like so many others before it and following Mass in Fatima, Lucia and her cousins met at the barreiro, as they usually did, to choose a site from which to pasture their flocks. On this day, they selected a pasture of land belonging to her parents, a place called Cova da Iria. The distance from Lucia's home to this site was over a mile and the journey required that the children and their sheep cross a barren stretch of moorland where the sheep took every opportunity to graze along the way, making the journey that much longer.[37] The length of the journey seemed irrelevant, however, because since the last appearance of the Angel, the children were more somber, deeper in prayer and sacrifice, and less interested in playing, dancing, singing, picking flowers and chasing butterflies.

---

[37] Dos Santos, Sr. Lucia, Fatima in Lucia's Own Words. The Remembrances of Sister Lucia, 20th Edition, 2016, page 44.

12:00 NOON

At about Noon the three children arrived high up on the slope in the Cova da Iria, a pasture containing little more than a spattering of assorted trees. There, the sheep continued to graze[38] and the children busied themselves gathering some of the scattered rocks to build a little stone wall that they could use as an enclosure around a clump of furze on which the sheep grazed. Suddenly a bright shaft of light pierced the air. It was so bright that it appeared to the children as a flash of lightning. Frightened by the flash, Lucia suggested that they make their way home to avoid the oncoming storm. Despite the clear sun-drenched sky, and with the absence of even a hint of a breeze, the children began to descend the hill hurrying the sheep along towards the road. When about halfway down the hill, almost level with a large holm oak tree that stood there, there was another flash of lightning. Now, even more alarmed, the children continued to scurry down the slope. They had moved only about another hundred yards when they came upon a small holm oak directly in front of them. Looking up the children saw a figure standing over the foliage of the small tree. According to Lucia, "a Lady dressed all in white, more brilliant than the sun, shedding rays of light, clear and stronger than a crystal glass filled with the most sparkling water, pierced the burning rays of the sun."

The cork oak, and not the holm oak, is a tree more typically found in Portugal. The holm oak is a very tall evergreen that grows up to 85 feet in height despite its turgid, grey, short and winding stem. It has alternating, very hard, elliptical bright green leaves that are whiter below. It produces yellow flowers and a green acorn that is very bitter to the taste and turns dark brown at maturity. The tree over which the figure stood, however, was apparently a very young tree, rather small in size reaching only about three feet in height.

The children stopped in their tracks just feet from the Lady. Her face was beautiful, indescribably so, bearing neither a smile nor a frown, but rather appearing very serious. She seemed to be about seventeen.[39] Around Her neck was a chord that fell to about the waist at the end of which was a little ball of light. Her hands were clasped as in prayer and were held about breast high.

---

[38] Ibid

[39] McGlynn, Fr. Thomas, O.P., Vision of Fatima, Washington, DC., 1948. page 92

Rosary beads were draped around her fingers. She wore a simple tunic under a mantle or veil, each falling to her feet. The tunic had no collar and no cuffs. The mantle had a ray of sunlight all around it and displayed a star. There was no cincture or sash around the waist, although the tunic was drawn in at that point.[40]

The entire figure was a brilliant light, white light for the most part except the face and hands which appeared as a flesh-color light. Below the mantle a yellow light encircled her. The light that shone from the Lady, particularly from her face, was so fierce that the children could not stare without hurting their eyes. They were bathed in the light that radiated from her and astounded as they stood before the Apparition.

Without providing even a chance to allow the children to comprehend what they were seeing, the Lady spoke to them in a low, almost melodic voice, saying, *"'Do not be afraid. I will do you no harm.'* 'Where are you from?' Lucia asked. *'I am from Heaven,'* the beautiful lady replied, gently raising her hand towards the distant horizon. 'What do you want of me?' Lucia intoned. *'I came to ask you to come here for six months in succession, on the thirteenth day, at this same hour. Later on I will tell you who I am and what I want. Afterwards, I will return here yet a seventh time.'* Lucia asked, 'Shall I go to heaven too?' *'Yes, you will.'* 'And Jacinta?' *'She will go also.'* 'And Francisco?' *'He will go there too, but he must say many Rosaries.'* Lucia then remembered two of her friends who used to come to her house to learn weaving from her eldest sister. They had recently died and Lucia inquired, 'Is Maria das Neves in Heaven?' Maria was only sixteen when she died. *'Yes she is,'* the Lady answered. 'And Amelia?' Lucia continued. *'She is in purgatory until the end of the world."* Amelia was about 18-20 years old when she died. Then the Lady asked, *'Are you willing to offer yourselves to God and bear all the sufferings He wills to send you, as an act of reparation for the sins by which He is offended, and of supplication for the conversion of sinners?'* 'Yes, we are willing,' said Lucia. *'Then you are going to have much to suffer, but the grace of God will be your comfort.'* As She said these words, She opened her hands for the first time imparting on the children an intense light that streamed from her

---

[40] Ibid, pages 63-65

hands. The rays of that light seemed to penetrate their hearts and touch the innermost depths of their souls.

Then, as if moved by an inner feeling that was also communicated to them through the light, the children fell to their knees and silently repeated, "O most Holy Trinity, I adore You! My God, my God, I love You in the most Blessed Sacrament!"

A few moments passed and the Lady said, *'Pray the Rosary every day, in order to obtain peace for the world, and the end of the war.'* The Woman then began to serenely rise and moved eastward until she disappeared into the air. Just like that she was gone![41]

As the children walked home after the apparition, they recounted the splendor of the experience they had just shared. Unable to contain herself, little Jacinta kept breaking into enthusiastic exclamations saying, "Oh, what a beautiful Lady!" Lucia, however, recalled the hardships created when her other friends spoke openly about the vision of the boy and warned Jacinta that her enthusiasm might cause her to break the vow they made earlier to keep their visions secret causing her to tell others what had taken place this day. Jacinta, for her part, told Lucia not to worry and promised that she would tell no one.

Francisco and Jacinta returned home to a houseful of people, including their own siblings and their Uncle Antonio da Silva, but their parents, who had taken the carriage into town earlier that morning, had not yet returned home. Dinner cooked on the stove and the daylight began to fade when Jacinta, who meant to keep the secret, heard the sound of the carriage that signaled the return of her parents from the market where they had just purchased a pig. Jacinta ran to greet them hugging her mother at the knees as she exited the carriage. "Mother, I saw Our Lady today at Cova da Iria!" Olimpia laughed at what she assumed was a joke and brushed by to go into the house. But Jacinta followed close behind insisting that her story was true. She provided so much detail that Olimpia had to take her seriously. When her father came in from locking the newly-acquired pig in a shed, he sat by the fireplace and began to eat his supper. Olimpia sat beside him and recounted the story that Jacinta has shared. Manuel

---

[41] Dos Santos, Sr. Lucia, Fatima in Lucia's Own Words. The Remembrances of Sister Lucia, 20th Edition, 2016. page 174-176. Also, http://www.theholyrosary.org/fatimaapparitions.

wanted to hear the story from Jacinta's own lips and called her over. She happily told him exactly what she told Olimpia. Manuel turned to Francisco for confirmation, which was provided. Uncle Antonio looked at his brother-in-law saying, "Well, if the youngsters did see a lady dressed in white, who could it be but Our Lady?" Manuel knew in his heart that his children didn't lie. He also knew that they were not playing a prank on him. After weighing the two accounts of events offered by Francisco and Jacinta, and after a careful evaluation of their body language as they told their story, and knowing that his children did not even know some of the words they attributed to the Lady, he announced his belief, saying, "From the beginning of the world, Our Lady has appeared many times in various ways. If the world is wicked, it would be much more so but for many such happenings. The power of God is great. We don't know what this is, but it will turn out to be something.

MAY 14, 1917

Lucia awoke early on Monday morning and played under the fig tree until it was time to take the sheep to pasture. After some time, Lucia noticed her sister Maria approaching her and was taken aback when Maria said, "Oh, Lucia! I hear you have seen Our Lady at Cova da Iria. Is it true?" "Who told you," Lucia demanded. Maria recounted that some neighbors informed her how Jacinta told their aunt Olimpia. Lucia told Maria that she didn't say anything because she wasn't sure who the Lady was. "It was a pretty little woman" who wants us to go for six consecutive months to the Cova. Only then will she tell us who she is and what she wants, Lucia told her.

Maria wasn't buying any of it and returned to the house to tell Maria Rosa all that Lucia had told her. Lucia was promptly summoned to the house where her disbelieving parents grilled her with questions prior to Antonio's dismissal of the whole matter as "Silly woman's tales." Maria Rosa, however was quite disturbed and scolded Lucia. "To think I always brought my children up to speak the truth!" Maria Rosa lamented, "And now this one brings me a whopper like this!"[42]

Francisco and Jacinta meanwhile waited for Lucia to arrive at their meeting spot. Francisco couldn't wait to share with Lucia the news about Jacinta telling the secret. Unable to contain his excitement for another second, he ran to her the moment he saw her leading the sheep toward him, explaining as he did, how Jacinta had told her parents everything about the visions of the Lady the day prior. Jacinta listened silently as Francisco excitedly recounted nearly verbatim everything Jacinta said. Lucia was visibly upset. "You see, that's just what I thought would happen." Jacinta broke her silence. "There was something within me that wouldn't let me keep quiet," she said with tears in her eyes. "Well don't cry now and don't tell anything to anybody about what the Lady said to us," Lucia continued. "But I already told them," Jacinta said. "And what did you say?" Lucia asked. "I said that the Lady promised to take us to Heaven," Jacinta replied. Lucia was incredulous thinking about the hardships this would cause. "To think you told them that!" she said. Jacinta sobbed even more saying, "Forgive me. I won't tell anybody anything ever again!"[43]

Reaching their destination at the pasture, Jacinta took a seat on a rock falling deep in thought. Remembering that the Lady told them to say the Rosary and make sacrifices for the conversion of sinners, she decided to refrain from their usual play. "From now on," she informed the others, when we pray the Rosary, we must pray the whole Our Father and the whole Hail Mary." Then, referring to the sacrifices, asked, "How are we going to make them?"[44]

Francisco thought for a moment and offered, "Let's give our lunch to the sheep, and make the sacrifice of doing without it." In just a few minutes, their lunches were divided among the sheep who quickly diverted their attention from the grass on which they had been grazing. So on May 14, 1917, "the children fasted as strictly as the most austere Carthusian!"[45]

---

[42] Walsh, William Thomas, Our Lady of Fatima, Image Book, Doubleday Publishing, 1954. Pages 56-57, taken from Olimpia's account to Father DeMarchi pg.64.

[43] Dos Santos, Sr. Lucia, Fatima in Lucia's Own Words. The Remembrances of Sister Lucia, 20th Edition, 2016, Pages 44-45.

[44] Ibid, page 45.

[45] Ibid, page 45-46, (the reference is to a member of a monastic order founded by St. Bruno in 1086 near Grenoble, France.)

Recalling that the Lady also told them that many sinners go to hell, Jacinta asked Lucia about it. Lucia explained the concept of hell to Jacinta as Maria Rosa had explained it to her. "It's like a big deep pit of wild beasts," Lucia explained, "with an enormous fire in it – and that's where people go who commit sins and don't confess them. They stay there and burn forever!" Jacinta was intrigued with the concept of eternity. Her six-year old mind just could not grasp how something could go on forever without coming to an end.

For the balance of the day she obsessed about hell and asked Lucia a battery of questions. "And they never get out of there? But listen! Doesn't hell end after many, many years, then? Those people burning in hell, don't they ever die? And don't they turn into ashes? And if people pray very much for sinners, won't Our Lord get them out of there? And if they make sacrifices as well?" Finally, realizing there was no relief for the condemned souls, she relented, "Poor sinners! We have to pray and make many sacrifices for them!" Pondering the situation further Jacinta said, "How good Our Lady is! She has already promised to take us to Heaven!"

MAY 15 – 20, 1917

The word of the visions witnessed by the three children continued to spread throughout the village eventually reaching the parish priest who sent for the three children so that he could question them directly. Lucia and Francisco cooperated by answering the priest's questions, but Jacinta hardly spoke. When she did break her silence, it was only with great hesitance and difficulty. As they left for home, Lucia asked why she didn't answer any questions to which Jacinta responded, "Because I promised you never to tell anything to anybody again."

Not even questioning by the parish priest, however, quelled the village talk and with each passing day, Lucia's mother grew more and more upset at the things being said. Not even Maria Rosa's anger could assuage the excitement felt deep within by the children. While all three believed fervently in the word spoken by the Lady of their vision, Jacinta seemed most enthusiastic in her desire to carry out every request made by the Lady on that fateful day. She reminded the others frequently that at the offering of each and every sacrifice they must be sure to "tell Jesus that it's for the love of Him" that the sacrifice was being made. If at any time Lucia admitted that she failed to do so, Jacinta would say, "Then I'll tell Him." She would then join her hands, raise her eyes to heaven and say: "Oh Jesus, it is for the love of You, and for the conversion of sinners!"[46]

Francisco seemed to relish his solitude more and more. One day in May he slipped away from Jacinta and Lucia, climbing to the top of a tall rock formation. "You can't come up here," he yelled down upon being discovered, "Leave me alone."[47]

WEDNESDAY JUNE 13, 1917
APPROXIMATELY 5:00 AM

June 13th is the Feast of St. Anthony of Padua and for the faithful people of Aljustrel it is an important day. The Missa Cantata was being celebrated at St. Anthony's Church at precisely 8:00 AM and it promised to be a full church. Lucia brought the sheep to pasture before sunrise so she could be back in time to attend. After a "good while" she noticed her brother Antonio running across the field toward her, informing her as he did, that several people were at the house asking to speak with her. Antonio agreed to watch the sheep for her as Lucia ran home to see who it was that wanted so urgently to see her.

On arrival, Lucia found many people from places as far as Minde, Carrascos and Boleiros among other villages on the other side of the mountains. They had all heard of the May apparition and the believers and curious alike wanted to accompany the children to Cova da Iria to check it out for themselves. Lucia was annoyed, but promised to allow them to accompany her to the Cova after she returned from the 8:00 Mass in Fatima. The crowd waited in her yard, much to the chagrin of Maria Rosa and her two elder daughters who ridiculed them for their folly. They waited for two hours for Lucia to return and then waited a bit longer for Lucia to ready herself.

---

[46] Ibid, page 50
[47] Walsh, William Thomas, Our Lady of Fatima, Image Book, Doubleday Publishing, 1954. page 60.

11:00 AM

Lucia and the group of strangers finally departed for the Cova though Lucia felt very bitter. It was not so much any annoyance with the people that crowded the street, but rather the disdain and contempt she felt from her once loving family. Thinking back to the good times of the past as she walked along the dusty road, she wondered where the affection had gone. She began to cry as the strangers peppered her with many questions. Finally, she reached her cousins' house.

Seeing Lucia's red eyes and wet cheeks, Jacinta tried to reassure her with a reminder that "Surely these must be the sacrifices that the Angel said God was going to send us. That is why you suffer – and to make reparation to Him, and to convert sinners!" Jacinta always had a way of putting things in perspective for Lucia who dried her eyes. The children and the strangers continued their thirty-minute or so journey to the Cova. Upon their arrival, the children were surprised to find another group of about fifty people waiting for them. This too was a diverse group from "Loureira, a little man from Lomba de Equa, others from Boleiros, Torres Novas, Anteiro; and then there was Maria Carreira and her daughters from Moita."[48]

At forty-six years of age, Maria Carreira, also known as Maria da Capelinha was married and had several children. She had been planning this trip for weeks after learning of the May apparitions from her husband who had been weeding a garden with Lucia's father. It was just two or three days following the apparition that Antonio told Mr. Carreira who thought it was nonsense. While he didn't believe it, he did bring the tale home to Maria who had a very different reaction. The Carreira's had a crippled son John, who was "hunchbacked, with knees that crossed and knocked together as he walked." Maria hoped for a cure for little John and vowed to make the pilgrimage to the Cova.

---

[48] Walsh, William Thomas, Our Lady of Fatima, Image Book, Doubleday Publishing, 1954. page 66.

JUST BEFORE NOON

Lucia and her cousins approached the holm oak, stopping about nine feet short of it. Facing east, they sat to wait, Jacinta on one side of Lucia and Francisco on the other. Many in the group also sat and some passed bread and wine. The children refused the bread but did accept oranges that they held in their hands. Perhaps because of boredom or, possibly just to take her mind off the large crowd, Jacinta started to play, but on rather short order, Lucia made her stop. The low din of the crowd was disrupted by a girl from Boleiros who started praying loudly the prayers in her prayer book.

When she finished, the group completed five decades of the Rosary and the girl from Baleiros began to recite the Litany of Our Lady. Lucia stopped her though pointing out the lack of sufficient time. Then, as if startled by a revelation, Lucia stood and yelled, "Jacinta, there comes Our Lady! There is the light!"[49] The children ran to the foot of the holm oak tree, and the group of people followed closely. The entire assembly knelt, some on the bushes and the gorse. The children looked upon the Face of Our Lady who once again stood upon the holm oak tree. Some in the crowd were close enough to witness the branches at the top of the tree bend and curve as if under pressure. Others noted that the sun dimmed even though the sky was without clouds.

Lucia raised her hands toward the sky and broke the silence. "Your Excellency told me to come here, please say what you want of me" *"I wish you to come here the 13th of next month; to pray the Rosary every day, and to learn to read. Later, I will tell you what I want."*

Maria Carreira could not understand what Our Lady was saying, but could hear "something like a very faint voice." [50] Lucia's sisters Maria and Teresa were also among the one hundred or so observers. Maria heard, along with some around her, what sounded like "a bee buzzing around inside an iron jar." She turned to Teresa with an inquisitive look, but Teresa heard nothing. She could see the children staring intently above the tree, but didn't observe its

---

[49] Walsh, William Thomas, Our Lady of Fatima, Image Book, Doubleday Publishing, 1954. page 67.
[50] Ibid.

branches bent in any particular way. She did, however, notice that Lucia was "talking and listening as one does in conversation."[51]

In response to a request she had received from one of the villagers, Lucia asked the Lady if she would cure a sick person. *"If he is converted, he will be cured during the year, the Lady promised."* "I would like to ask you to take us to Heaven," Lucia said. *'Yes, I will take Jacinta and Francisco soon. But you are to stay here some time longer. Jesus wishes to make use of you to make me known and loved. He wants to establish in the world a devotion to my Immaculate Heart. I promise salvation to those who embrace it, and those souls will be loved by God like flowers placed by me to adorn His throne."* Lucia asked sadly: "Am I to stay here alone?" *"No my daughter. Are you suffering a great deal? Don't lose heart. I will never forsake you. My Immaculate Heart will be your refuge and the way that will lead you to God."*

Upon speaking these final words, the Lady opened her hand and for the second time emanated her light on the children. Lucia noted that the light was a form of communication in which the children saw themselves immersed in God. "Jacinta and Francisco seemed to be in that part of the light that rose towards Heaven," while Lucia remained in the "light which was poured out on the earth. In front of the palm of Our Lady's right hand was a heart encircled by thorns which pierced it. The children instinctively understood that this was the Immaculate Heart of Mary, outraged by the sins of humanity, and for which they must seek reparation. Within the vision of the Most Blessed Trinity the children could see Jesus and Mary.[52]

As the vision of the Trinity faded and Our Lady spoke these final words, She ascended from the holm oak tree and quickly floated away toward the east until She was no longer visible. Maria Carreira heard Lucia say, "Pronto! Now she can't be seen any more. Now she is entering heaven, Now the doors are being shut."[53]

---

[51] McGlynn, Fr. Thomas, O.P., Vision of Fatima, Washington, DC., 1948, page 47

[52] Dos Santos, Sr. Lucia, Fatima in Lucia's Own Words. The Remembrances of Sister Lucia, 20th Edition, 2016. pages 176-177. Also, http://www.theholyrosary.org/fatimaapparitions.

[53] Walsh, William Thomas, Our Lady of Fatima, Image Book, Doubleday Publishing, 1954. page 69

The children remained as they were but the people assembled to witness the event were very excited. Though they could see nothing, it was apparent to them that something amazing had just happened. Some argued about what took place while others asked questions of the children. Still others began to pluck leaves from the top of the tree forcing Lucia to ask them to take only the leaves from the bottom, those not touched by Our Lady.

4:00 PM

Many within the assemblage finally dispersed in different directions reciting the Rosary as they departed. The children too were now able to make their way back to Aljustrel with just a few of the crowd still following them asking questions and taunting them. Discouraged at the lack of reply, the last of the strangers departed leaving the children in peace. Now it was Francisco's turn to ask questions. For as with the previous apparitions, he could see, but not hear the words of Our Lady. Lucia explained that Jacinta and Francisco would go to heaven soon which caused Francisco a great deal of excitement.

When they reached their house Jacinta and Francisco ran in very excitedly. Manual and Olimpia had just returned home from the fair where they purchased two oxen. The other children had attended the St. Anthony festivities at Fatima. "We saw the Lady again Mother!" Jacinta exclaimed. "And she told me that I am going to heaven soon." Olimpia and her siblings questioned her in disbelief, almost mockingly, but their father neither laughed at his two youngest children nor tried to pry from them the secrets Our Lady shared with them.

Lucia's reception upon her arrival home was a bit more chilling. Her family were already convinced that she was an unconscionable liar and Maria Rosa was becoming increasingly more indignant. She ridiculed the crowd of onlookers calling them fools and blamed Lucia for the hysteria.

JUNE 14 – JULY 11, 1917

The days passed but not without the suffering that Our Lady had promised would be experienced by the children. The villagers all seemed to have turned against them. They laughed at them and ridiculed them at virtually every opportunity. The children became the brunt of the villagers' jokes and to some, the object of their hatred. Yet, that did not bother Lucia nearly as much as the betrayal she felt from her sisters and mother. Reaching the boiling point Maria Rosa told Lucia that in the morning they were again going to go see Fr. Ferreira at St. Anthony's and at that time Lucia would tell him the truth!

The two set out for St. Anthony's Church early the next morning with a sullen Lucia walking several feet behind her determined mother. When they reached the Marto house, Maria Rosa stopped in to speak with Olimpia providing a few moments for Lucia to meet with Jacinta. In her calming way Jacinta told Lucia not to cry but instead to offer it as a sacrifice adding that she and Francisco would go to the well to pray for her and told Lucia to join them as soon as she returned.

Lucia and her mother continued up the hill toward the church without speaking a word. Maria Rosa never glanced back at Lucia and her every step, as well as her black dress, dark shawl and black kerchief betrayed the anger that she harbored. Prior to going to see the pastor, however, Maria Rosa entered the church and attended the Holy Mass providing some much-needed relief for the forlorn Lucia. Kneeling before the uplifted Host and Chalice, the seer offered all her sufferings to her Lord and Savior. The Mass ended far too soon for Lucia's liking and the two were off to the rectory. About midway up the stairs leading to the front door, Maria Rosa turned to Lucia, acknowledging her for the first time since they left home, saying, "Don't annoy me anymore! Tell the Prior now that you lied, so that on Sunday he can say in the church that it was a lie, and end the whole thing before all the people go running to Cova da Iria to pray in front of a holm oak bush!"[54] Fr. Ferreira invited them in and the two had a seat until the Pastor called for Lucia to join him in his study. There he asked her many questions, every detail, even the most boring. He had already spoken to Francisco and Jacinta so he had fairly good information with which to make a comparison of Lucia's detail. After thoughtful analysis, Fr. Ferreira determined that the children had told the truth about what they had seen and heard. But, he added, "It doesn't seem to me like a revelation from heaven. It

[54] Walsh, William Thomas, Our Lady of Fatima, Image Book, Doubleday Publishing, 1954. page 74.

may be a deception of the devil, you know! We shall see. We shall see. We shall give our opinion later on," he said to Maria Rosa as they departed the rectory.

This startling revelation took Lucia and her mother aback. The poor little girl was exhausted and terrified. On the return walk home, Maria Rosa took every opportunity to remind Lucia of the words of the priest and sometimes added blows and kicks for emphasis. As soon as they arrived home, Lucia retreated to the solace of the well where she had seen the Angel. There she found Francisco and Jacinta still on their knees praying for their cousin. Jacinta ran to Lucia asking how the meeting went. They listened with indignation as Lucia told them everything. "It's not the devil," Jacinta objected. "No! They say the devil is very foul and ugly, and he is under the ground in hell. And that Lady is so beautiful, and we saw her go up to heaven!"[55]

Despite Jacinta's reassurance, Lucia was unable to sleep at all that night, replaying the words of the priest in her mind repeatedly, and wondering if it was possible that she had unwittingly become the instrument of Satan. This mental anguish repeated itself each night for a very long time and Lucia's suffering was great.

JULY 12, 1917

The constant berating of her family, the anguish caused by her nightmares and the horrific thoughts generated by her own imagination were too much for Lucia. She finally determined that the priest must be right and that her visions had to be the work of the devil. She informed Francisco and Jacinta that she would not accompany them to the Cova da Iria the following day as previously instructed by the Lady. Her two young cousins made several attempts to convince her to go to the Cova with them, but Lucia was steadfast in her commitment to never again go to the Cova da Iria on the 13th of the month.

Yet, there was something deep within her that caused her concern. After all, even the hardships of her newfound daily life delivered some consolations. Her mind drifted to the day when two priests visited her, encouraged her,

---

[55] Ibid, page 76.

and asked her to pray for the Holy Father. "Who is the Holy Father?" Lucia inquired. The priest took great pains to explain who the Holy Father was and his role in the faith. From that day forward, Lucia and her cousins never missed an opportunity to pray for him adding three Aves to their daily Rosary for the Vicar of Christ.

And there was the terrific example of Francisco, who not only embraced his sufferings, but seemed to enjoy them. He would frequently say, "That doesn't matter to me, I will suffer everything as much as she wants!" He would even provide comfort to Lucia at her lowest moments reminding her, "Didn't Our Lady say we should have much to suffer?"[56]

Finally, overcome with mental exhaustion from the endless mind games, Lucia drifted off to sleep.

SATURDAY JULY 13, 1917

When Lucia awoke she was still determined to refrain from taking the sheep to the Cova that day. This apparently pleased Maria Rosa, though her relief would be short-lived. As the hour drew near to take the sheep from the coral, Lucia was overcome with a desire to see her cousins. She rushed to their house only to find them kneeling beside a bed crying. "Aren't you going," Lucia asked them. "We don't dare go without you!" they sobbed as their tears fell gently to the floor. "Well, I've changed my mind, and I'm going," Lucia informed them. Overjoyed, Francisco told Lucia that they have been praying all night that she might relent in her stubbornness.

Despite the oppressive heat of July, the children ran almost the entire two plus miles of dusty road on their way to the Cova. It hadn't rained in weeks and the scorching sun drenched the earth making it almost impossible for the laborers to pick the plums or harvest their potatoes. None of the efforts of those struggling roadside laborers was even noticed by the children, however, as they approached the Cova.

Some two to three thousand people had already gathered there including Maria Carriera and her entire family; even her disbelieving husband and

---

[56] Ibid, pages 59-60.

their crippled son. Also present for today's anticipated apparition was Jose Alves of Moita who had informed Fr. Ferreira that his theory of these apparitions being the deceit of the devil was an impossibility. "Who ever heard of the devil inciting people to pray?" the good man had inquired of his priest.

Even Manuel Marto had decided to take the day off to see for himself what his children obsessed about, but found navigation through the dense crowd of onlookers most difficult. He finally reached Jacinta and laughed to himself thinking of the outfits that some of the people he had just passed were wearing; men in their Sunday suits and women barefoot dressed all in black. He also was a bit concerned at the size of the crowd thinking for the first time that the safety of his children might be at risk. Manuel even noticed his wife and sister-in-law Maria Rosa in the crowd clutching a supply of matches and some holy candles as if ready to perform some type of exorcism.

Manuel took his place next to his children who had not even noticed his arrival. They were kneeling, totally consumed with leading the crowd in the Rosary. As they prayed the three seers first witnessed the flash of light approach. Lucia glanced over and noticed for the first time her uncle and other men wearing hats. "Take off your hats! Take off your hats, for I see Our Lady already!" A moment later, the children saw the Lady upon the holm oak tree. Manuel looked up and noticed a small cloud come to rest over the tree, but before he could acknowledge it or figure out what it might be, the sunlight seemed to dim. A cool breeze blew and he heard a buzz, what he thought sounded "like a horse-fly in an empty water pot." Maria Carriera heard it too, but only Lucia and Jacinta could understand the words Our Lady was speaking to them.[57]

Lucia again, as she had in the previous apparitions, was the first to speak. "What do you want from me?" she said. The Lady answered, *"I want you to come here. That you come the 13th of next month, to continue to pray the Rosary every day in honor of Our Lady of the Rosary, in order to obtain peace for the world and the end of the war, because only She can help you."* Lucia then said, 'I would like to ask you to tell us who you are, and to work a miracle so that everybody will believe that you are appearing to us." She answered, *"Continue to come here every month. In October, I will tell you who I am and*

---

[57] Ibid, pages 79-80.

what I want, and I will perform a miracle for all to see and believe." Lucia then made a number of requests of the Lady, petitions that were requested of her by others for healings. There were many but among them was a request for a cure for Maria Carreira's crippled son to which the Lady responded that she would not cure him but would give him a means of livelihood if he would say his Rosary every day. She noted that all such people needed to pray the Rosary in order to obtain the graces needed during the year for their requests to be granted. *"Sacrifice yourselves for sinners,"* the Lady continued, *"and say many times, especially whenever you make some sacrifice: Oh Jesus, it is for love of you, for the conversion of sinners, and in reparation for the sins committed against the Immaculate Heart of Mary."*

As she spoke these words, Our Lady stretched out her hands, as before, emulating rays of light that seemed to penetrate directly into the earth, exposing to the children a sea of fire. In Lucia's words, "Plunged in this fire were demons and souls in human form, like transparent burning embers, all blackened or burnished bronze, floating about in the conflagration, now raised into the air by the flames that issued from within themselves together with great clouds of smoke now falling back on every side like sparks in huge fires, without weight or equilibrium, amid shrieks and groans of pain and despair."

The vision horrified the children and made then tremble with fear causing Lucia to cry out. "The demons could be distinguished by their terrifying and repellent likeness to frightful and unknown animals, black and transparent like burning coals. Terrified and as if to plead for succor," the children looked up at the Lady, who so kindly, and ever so sadly, said to them,

> *"You have seen Hell where the souls of poor sinners go. To save them, God wishes to establish in the world devotion to My Immaculate Heart. If what I say to you is done, many souls will be saved and there will be peace. The war is going to end, but if people do not cease offending God, a worse one will break out during the pontificate of Pius XI. When you see the night illumined by an unknown light, know that this is the great sign given you by God that he is about to punish the world for its crimes, by means of war, famine, and persecutions of the Church and of the Holy Father. To prevent this, I*

shall come to ask for the consecration of Russia to my Immac-
ulate Heart, and the Communion of Reparation on the First
Saturdays. If my requests are heeded, Russia will be converted
and there will be peace. If not, she will spread her errors
throughout the world, causing wars and persecution of the
Church. The good will be martyred, the Holy Father will have
much to suffer, various nations will be annihilated. In the end,
my Immaculate Heart will triumph. The Holy Father will con-
secrate Russia to me, and she will be converted, and a period
of peace will be granted to the world. Do not tell this to any-
body. Francisco, yes, you may tell him. When you pray the
Rosary, say after each mystery, 'Oh my Jesus, forgive us, save
us from the fire of hell. Lead all souls to Heaven, especially
those who are in most need.'"

The Lady then revealed the third and final secret. In the moments that followed not a sound could be heard, not even from the two to three thousand assembled until Lucia broke the silence by asking, "Is there anything more that you want of me?" Being nothing else, the Lady ascended towards the east disappearing into the "immense distance of the firmament." [58]

The children remained silently staring eastward for a time and then looked at each other as people began to close in around them. "What did she look like? What did she say? The questions seemed never ending. Manuel grabbed his daughter pulling her up in his arms. She hugged his neck as the people continued to barrage her and the other children with questions. And so it went until someone offered to take them home in an automobile. Mr. Marto agreed and the exhausted children rushed into the waiting car and headed for home. [59]

---

[58] Ibid. Also, http://www.theholyrosary.org/fatimaapparitions.
[59] Ibid, page 82-83.

THE DAYS PRIOR TO AUGUST 10, 1917

As August 13, 1917 approached, word of the Fatima apparitions spread throughout the region far beyond the confines of Fatima. The anti-Catholic secular newspapers began to pick up coverage of the story and conspiracy theories were plentiful. The *Jacobin*, for example, questioned whether the entire affair was a theatrical event staged by the clergy, particularly the Jesuits, as a means of regaining some of the prestige lost in the Revolution of 1910. *O Seculo*, Lisboa's chief secular daily, printed a "sarcastic and distorted account on July 21, 1917, under the headline:

A MESSAGE FROM HEAVEN-COMMERCIAL SPECULATION?

Even the Catholic diocesan paper *The Ouriense of Ourem*, was careful in their acknowledgement of a miracle. That headline read:

REAL APPARITION OR SUPPOSED ILLUSION

Many sought some scientific explanation for the reported apparitions raising psychosis, epilepsy and collective suggestion as possible explanations of the incredible tale from the Serra da Aire.[60]

While not being able to read the newspaper accounts, the children were put out by the spectacle of people; self-serving people who came from miles in carriages and automobiles, dressed in fancy clothes, who were there, for the most part, to see what bounty they might claim from heaven's messengers. They were more tolerant of the poor who walked miles, without shoes, some completing the final mile on bleeding knees, to beg the children to intercede with Our Lady for a cure for some infirmed, diseased or crippled family member, but even for them the children's patience was being stretched thin. Manuel Marto remembers the insane questions that some people asked, some of them were terrible. "Did Our Lady also have goats and sheep when she was a little girl? Did Our Lady ever eat potatoes?"

---

[60] Ibid, page 84.

The questions were constant coming from all directions. The children could have no rest when someone of these strangers was around.

Children are resilient and the three visionaries of Fatima were not any different in that regard as they became quite skilled at avoiding curiosity seekers. One day, when they saw several well-to-do ladies and gentlemen emerge from an automobile, the children knew there was no escape for they had already been spotted. "Where do the little shepherds live? The ones that saw Our Lady?" they asked. The children gave very exact directions to their homes and the strangers thanked them, climbed back into their automobile, and drove down the hill. The children were excited at their accomplishment and hid among some olive trees behind Lucia's house until they thought it safe to emerge.

The children were especially fearful of priests who traveled to see them. Many were Jesuits and they had a propensity for treating the children with skepticism and hostility. They seem almost trained to ask many clever questions that others would never think to ask, questions meant to trick them or trip them up to prove that they were lying.

The exception was the saintly Fr. Cruz, the same man who told Fr. Pena that Lucia was versed enough in her catechism to receive her First Communion despite her young age, later telling Lucia, "My daughter, our soul is the temple of the Holy Spirit. Keep it always pure…" But that was four years earlier. So much had happened since that time of cherished innocence. Fr. Cruz changed too. He was nearly crippled and found that walking had become a most difficult exercise. Despite his pain, he continued to preach and save souls.

He questioned the children in a most respectful way and then asked them to lead him to the exact spot of the apparitions. The children walked on either side as the good priest rode a small donkey along the road. It was for him, as well as the children, an arduous journey, but a trip well worth the sacrifice as Fr. Cruz concluded after his questions and site visit, that the children had told the truth of what they had witnessed. He taught them many prayers meant to console them and from that moment became a champion of their visions.

Lucia's family however, remained unconvinced and grew in their hostility toward Lucia. Even Antonio, once more ambivalent to his daughter's fantasies, now joined in his family's aggression after traveling to the Cova and witnessing the destruction that the crowds had caused to his land. His vegetable gardens were destroyed. The soil around them was so hard after being trampled by thousands of feet that any attempt at cultivation was useless. Horses had eaten his cabbage, beans and potato vines. What wasn't eaten was trampled. There would be no crops. The family feared starvation and Antonio began drinking even more than he had before.

Whenever Lucia was hungry, her sisters would tell her to go to the Cova da Iria and eat what she could find growing. Her mother told her to go ask "that Lady" for something to eat. Not even Jacinta could reason with her aunt and cousins as she tried to explain that it was not Lucia's fault that all these people went to Cova da Iria. It was too late; the die had been cast. It was only at the Cova or Valinhos or the hills near the Cova that Lucia could take any solace whatsoever.

The children continued to lament what Our Lady had them witness. The vision of hell was so vivid on their impressionable minds that they just couldn't stop thinking about it. It monopolized all their discussions and even made the solitude and peacefulness of time at the Cova more frightening. Francisco seemed to handle it best preferring to focus on the goodness of God. Jacinta could not. She began having visions of the future; of the horrors of World War II, of starving people lining a road crying with hunger, of the Holy Father kneeling in a church before the Immaculate Heart of Mary leading hundreds, maybe thousands in prayer. There was so much more about the Pope in Jacinta's visions that Lucia warned her not to speak of as it would violate Our Lady's request to keep the secrets She had imparted to the children.

The children were destined to walk along the path that Christ chose for them and Jacinta, at least, could see where the road was leading. The persecution that awaited Jesus on his chosen path of Calvary was in store for the three visionaries and the antagonism from many people that confronted them, the hatred of what they had become, was seemingly never ending. But the words of loathe were about to take on a new dimension as those words began to morph into the political action of the anti-clerical elite.

Administrator Artur de Oliveira Santos, Fatima's local authority, was headquartered in the district of Vila Nova de Ourem, and was every bit an anti-clerical fanatic as those in charge of the newspapers. Known as "The Tinsmith," owing to his former profession, the Administrator was a Freemason who enjoyed enormous power through his position, and ruled his district in a tyrannical style, "imposing restrictions on churches and religious services on his slightest whim." Now, he was hearing tales of two to three thousand people flocking to a place called Cova da Iria to hear three children converse with an invisible woman standing atop a small tree! He was out of patience and, in response to the mounting pressure from other anti-clerics, and what the various liberal newspaper editors called "an invasion of mysticism," he decided to bring about the end to the popular devotion that resulted from the shepherd's visions in Fatima. Worse, he vowed to accomplish this using whatever means necessary. He began by notifying the fathers of the three seers of Fatima, Manuel Marto and Antonio dos Santos, to appear with their children at Vila Nova de Ourem.[61]

Jacinta, (left) Lucia, (middle) and Francisco (right) pose for a photo in 1917. The three children suffered greatly following the first Apparition on May 13th. They were ridiculed, interrogated by clergy and government officials and threatened with a torturous death if they wouldn't recant their stories of the Marian Apparitions.

FRIDAY AUGUST 10, 1917

The Administrator's notice was delivered on August 10, 1917 and caught the children's fathers by complete surprise. Vila Nova de Ourem was a journey of about nine miles and the only way the summoned could make the trip was to walk or ride a donkey. Manuel Marto was upset with the imposition and refused to have his two young children make such an arduous journey, a position his wife Olimpia supported. Moreover, he was not going to have his

---

[61] http://www.fatima.org/essentials/opposed/seerkidn.asp

young children subjected to questioning before the court. He opted instead to make the journey without his children. Antonio dos Santos, however, wanted more than anything to put an end to the absurdity his daughter had created and insisted that Lucia would be present to answer for herself. Maria Rosa concurred. They, therefore, required her to make the extensive, time-consuming trek.

Lucia overheard the discussions and was bitter at the extreme reaction of her family. She lamented in conversation with Jesus, "Why would my aunt and uncle put themselves in danger to defend their children, but my parents turn me over with the greatest indifference, that they may do with me what they will. And she prayed to Him, "But patience! I expect to have to suffer more for Thy love, O my God, and it is for the conversion of sinners."[62]

SATURDAY AUGUST 11, 1917
MORNING

Antonio and Lucia set out for Ourem on Saturday in the early morning hours stopping by the Marto house along the way. The two fathers spoke for a bit giving Lucia a chance to seek out her cousin. Lucia cried to Jacinta recounting the conversation she had overheard at home. "Never mind," Jacinta said not even trying to disguise her fear. "If they kill you, you just tell them that I am like you, and Francisco even more so, and that we want to die too. And now I will go with Francisco to the well to pray very hard for you." They hugged and Lucia and her father resumed their long journey.[63]

---

[62] Walsh, William Thomas, Our Lady of Fatima, Image Book, Doubleday Publishing, 1954. Page 98 taken from Memoir II. Also, http://www.fatima.org/essentials/opposed/seerkidn.asp.

[63] Ibid, page 98.

NOON

Antonio and his daughter arrived in Ourem tired and hot after the long journey and made their way to the Administration building. Antonio was furious to find the building closed and the doors locked with not a soul in site. The searing heat added to his frustration as he and Lucia made their way along the cobblestone road looking for anyone that might be able to direct them to the Tinsmith. Instead they stumbled upon Manuel who had just arrived on his horse. Antonio conveyed his frustration and Manuel suggested that, because of the hour, they get a bite to eat before trying to find the Administrator. After lunch, the three made their way back to the Administration building only to learn that the building was still closed-up tightly. They stood commiserating for a while until, eventually, a man sauntered by and informed them that the Administration Building had moved to a different street for which he provided directions. The tired travelers made their way as instructed.

Shortly thereafter Antonio, Lucia and Manuel arrived at their destination. The Tinsmith studied his "guests" but seemed more interested in who was absent than those present. "And the boy," he demanded. "What boy," Manuel replied, realizing that the Administrator didn't know that there was a third child missing. Manuel feigned ignorance that his "child's" presence had been required, but the Administrator voiced his displeasure rather loudly.

In the absence of his other anticipated witness, de Oliveira Santos focused his entire attention on poor Lucia, vigorously interrogating her in the presence of not only her father and her uncle, but several other men unknown to Lucia. The Administrator was determined to force her to reveal the Secret disclosed by the Lady and to extract Lucia's promise to never again return to the Cova da Iria. To attain his objective the Tinsmith spared neither promise nor threat. Despite his efforts, he could accomplish nothing as Lucia remained silent except to recount, for what seemed to her the hundredth time, the events that were previously disclosed. Seeing that he was getting nowhere with Lucia, he turned to her father. "You there, do they believe these things over in Fatima?" "Oh, no sir!" Antonio replied, "All this is just women's tales." Turning to her uncle the Tinsmith said, "And you, what do you say?" If Manuel had any fear he did not show it. Standing tall he answered, "I am here at your command

* * *

and my children say the same things I do." "Then you think it's true," the Administrator demanded. "Yes, sir," Manuel answered, "I believe what they say." At that, the Administrator dismissed them vowing, however, that he would achieve his end, even if this meant that he had to take Lucia's life.[64]

The three headed back to Aljustrel arriving late in the day and Lucia headed straight for the well where she found her faithful cousins kneeling in prayer. Jacinta ran to Lucia and held her tightly saying, "Your sister told us they had killed you!" They all laughed and enjoyed their reunion as the Angel's lamps began to twinkle in the evening sky.

SUNDAY AUGUST 12, 1917

Crowds had already begun to gather in Fatima many carrying baskets of food, jugs of water, even blankets on which to sleep in the fields for the night. They searched for the children to bring their petitions of the Blessed Mother. Cures, money, love, and jobs. Just about anything imaginable. Some were from faraway places. Others, local villagers, but all sought out the children in relentless fashion.

Maria Rosa was furious, mostly at Lucia, whose "lie" caused this steady onslaught of people that ruined her fields and trampled her crops. If not for her promise to Our Lady to be at the Cova on Monday, Lucia may have accepted her Aunt Cascais offer to keep Lucia and her cousins sheltered at her house until the crowds dwindled. No, Lucia needed to stay home and endure the suffering for the conversion of sinners.

The crowds were rough, treating the children less like people than objects. The people meant no malice, but simply became overexcited when they saw the children. Lucia noted "In the hands of those people we were like a ball in the hands of a little girl. Each one pulled us in his direction and asked his question, without ever giving us time to answer anybody."

By early evening, three policemen arrived at Antonio and Maria Rosa's home, not to quell the noisy crowd that pressed in around their house, but rather

---

[64] Ibid, pages 99-100. Also, http://www.fatima.org/essentials/opposed/seerkidn.asp.

to deliver a summons for Lucia to go to the Marto house where the Administrator waited for her. Lucia's father actually received the notification and it was he who took the frightened child to her aunt's house.

At the home of Manuel and Olimpia Marto the Administrator was already threatening the children with death if they persisted in their silence. "Never mind," Jacinta said softly to Francisco, "If they kill us, so much the better, for then we will see Jesus and Our Lady." The lengthy interrogation that followed Lucia's arrival produced no better outcome for Administrator de Oliveira Santos, who, though frustrated, cleverly realized that a different approach would be necessary if he were to have any success in extracting the "secrets" departed to the children by the Lady.

Over the course of the next few hours, the Tinsmith concocted a new scheme. If the children would not agree to his demands that they reveal their secret and not return to Cova da Iria, then he would use his immense power to extract the information and prevent them from ever returning to the site of the visions. Noting that Father Ferreira would be a more appropriate person to involve himself in matters of this sort, the Administrator asked if the children's parents would object "to their going to the rectory next morning before keeping their rendezvous at Cova da Iria. Fatima, after all, was on the way to the place of the apparition." Securing their agreement, the Administrator departed.

MONDAY AUGUST 13, 1917
EARLY MORNING

Early the next morning, de Oliveira Santos arrived at the Marto house where Lucia had already joined her two cousins. He was not expected as Manuel assumed he, not the Administrator, would take his children to the rectory. But as he stood in the doorway, the Administrator informed Manuel that he too wanted to witness the miracle and that they could all go together to the rectory and then the Cova. Manuel was suspicious. This was uncharacteristic behavior for the Administrator. Besides, he looked awfully nervous for someone of his command. "Let's all go together," the Tinsmith said, "I will take the little ones with me in the wagon. See and believe like Saint Thomas! Where are the children, by the way? Time is getting on. You'd better have them called."[65] As the children entered the room the Administrator informed them of his plan. Despite their hesitance, he convinced them that they should go with him. "We'll have more time to stop at Fatima, at the house of the Prior. He wants to ask them some questions, you know!" Not even Manuel could overcome that logic with an objection, and the children climbed into the Official's wagon. Francisco sat in the front and the two girls in back. Manuel and Antonio followed on foot as St. Anthony's Church and rectory were just a few minutes away at the top of the hill.

On arrival, the Administrator called for Lucia to enter the rectory first while the other two waited in the wagon. Fr. Ferreira's formerly accepting demeanor seemed to change, however, when he questioned Lucia on this day. "Who taught you to say the things that you are going about saying?" the priest inquired. "That Lady whom I saw at Cova da Iria," Lucia responded compliantly. "Anyone who goes around spreading such wicked lies as the lies you tell will be judged, and will go to hell if it isn't true. More and more, many people, are being deceived by you," the priest warned. Lucia remained respectful albeit forceful in her reply. "If anyone who lies goes to hell, I will not go to hell," Lucia retorted as she stared directly into the priest's eyes, "for I don't lie and I tell only what I have seen and what the Lady has said to me. And as for the crowd that goes there, they only go because they want to. We don't' call anybody."[66]

APPROXIMATELY 11:00 AM

Fr. Ferreira then tried to extract from Lucia the secret that was told to the children by the Lady. "I can't tell it. But if Your Reverence wants to know it, I will ask the Lady, and if she gives me permission, I will tell you." The Administrator interrupted at this point noting that these are "supernatural" matters that wasted his time. He took Lucia and departed the rectory, ordering Lucia back into the wagon and headed down the road toward Ourem, a direction

---

[65] Ibid, page 103.
[66] Ibid, page 104

opposite that of the Cova. To Lucia's objection he rather cheerfully noted, "It's all right, we'll stop and see the Prior at Ourem a moment. Then I'll take you to Cova da Iria by automobile. You'll be there in time!"[67]

To hide the children from the crowds that made their way in large numbers to the Cova, the Administrator covered them with blankets. Lucia's father and uncle, who had no idea where the Administrator was taking their children, continued on foot to follow the wagon until they lost sight of it. They then turned and joined the crowd walking toward Cova da Iria. When they finally reached their destination some 30 minutes later, they found over 6,000 people assembled, people who arrived on foot, horseback, mule, bicycle, carriage and automobile. All asked for the children as the hour drew close to Noon.

Among the faithful and curious was Maria Carreira who had prepared a special table with flowers as an "altar" to Our Lady. She had also "supervised the erection of a rustic arch, with some crosses tied to it, and two hanging lamps to mark the spot at night. It seems incredible and most inconsistent with her former and future attitude toward her daughter's visionary claims, but Maria Rosa is said to have contributed something toward these lamps; and her oldest daughter was helping to arrange the arch and the table."[68]

12:00 NOON

The children were conspicuously absent from the Cova, but some of the large crowd gathered around the holm oak tree on which Our Lady was expected to appear and knelt to say the Rosary. Eventually, the entire crowd joined in. At that point, a faint "murmuring sound was heard, followed by what seemed to be a rumble of thunder, some thought in the road, others in the little tree, still others on the far horizon."

Some in the crowd grew frightened as they placed some credence in a rumor that spread regarding the apparitions being the devil's work. It seems that there is a "small, extinct volcanic crater near the Cova da Iria…and," some believed, "that it [the story of the apparitions] was all a trick of the devil to get

---

[67] Ibid
[68] Ibid, page 105.

these good people in one place, and then have it open up and swallow them in its fiery depths."[69] So at the sound of the thunder, some ran away in fear while others seemed paralyzed in their fear. "We're all going to die," a few of the terrified were heard saying. Those who remained noticed a flash of light and what appeared to be a small white cloud approaching from the east and settling over the holm oak tree. Just a few seconds later, it rose from the tree and drifted eastward into the blue sky. As the onlookers glanced at one another they noticed that their faces and clothing were "tinted with the various colors of the rainbow…while the foliage of the trees and bushes seemed like brilliant flowers instead of leaves, and the dry earth itself was checkered with different gorgeous hues. There is no doubt Our Lady had come," Maria Carreira commented, "but she didn't find the children."[70]

It seems that different people witnessed slightly different events that day although each description was similar, if not exact, in nature. Lucia's sisters Maria and Teresa, who were also present at this time described their experience. They could see that the crowd was growing impatient. Their father, Antonio, yelled to the assembled that there was no need to wait as the children were not present. On short order, there was a loud noise. Some reacted to the sound of what Teresa described as two sticks banging together. Maria didn't hear it, but those who did grew frightened and started to run up the north slope of the Cova. Maria and Teresa were unsure what they were running from, but followed anyway. As they ran, Maria heard an old man say, "People of little faith, don't' you see the miracle?" Maria and Teresa stopped and walked back toward the man, and they too noticed something unusual. "flowers resembling snow falling from the sky, and colored lights like a rainbow on the ground. People put out their hands to catch the flowers only to find that they disappeared." [71]The clouds around the sun also "reflected different colors on the people." Some saw "the figure of Our Lady in the clouds," but Maria and Teresa did not.

Many wondered what had happened to them and though neither of the fathers revealed anything of the morning's events, rumor began to circulate through the crowd that Fr. Ferreira and the Administrator were responsible to

---

[69] Ibid

[70] Ibid

[71] McGlynn, Fr. Thomas, O.P., Vision of Fatima, Washington, DC, 1948, Page 43, 47-48

the children's absence. The crowd grew hostile toward them shouting, "Down with the Administrator, Down with the Prior!" Some in the crowd suggested taking a mob to Fatima, if not Ourem, to deal with the scoundrels face to face, until reminded that justice will be administered by God and should not be left to man's discretion. Manuel Marto, however, was more concerned about the well-being of his children and hastily returned home where he found his wife weeping.

To Lucia, Francisco and Jacinta, it was abundantly clear that the Tinsmith had no intention of taking them to the priest's house as he drove them directly to his house. Once there, the children were taken to a room and told that they would not be let out until they had revealed the Secret. The children were certainly frightened, but despite the terror they were most concerned that they missed their appointment with Our Lady. Francisco hoped out loud that the Lady would make an appearance there in the room, but there was no flash of light, no approaching cloud, no sign of Our Lady. The three of them wondered if their absence made the Lady sad and discussed whether she might ever appear to them again. Jacinta cried as Francisco did his best to console her. "Let's offer this to Jesus for poor sinners, as that Lady told us to do," he said. And turning his eyes toward heaven, he began to pray. Jacinta soon joined with Francisco in prayer and night turned to morning.

AUGUST 14, 1917
10:00 AM

The Administrator came to the room where the children were being held and led them to the Town Hall, there, conducting another long inquisition. But the night of captivity did nothing to loosen the children's tongues. The frustrated Administrator concluded his questioning after a couple of hours and began to think of his options.

12:00 NOON

By lunchtime the children found themselves back at the Administrator's home where they were given lunch by the Tinsmith's kind wife who felt compassion for them. She even let them play with her children for a time, seeing to it that they lacked for nothing. Lucia noticed how her little cousin continued to suffer with the realization that their parents had abandoned them. With tears streaming down her cheeks, Jacinta said, "Neither your parents nor mine have come to see us. They don't bother about us anymore!"

With little regard to his wife's expression of compassion, the Administrator was determined to extract from the children the confession that would put an end to the nonsense once and for all. He questioned the children a bit more, and gaining no information, informed them that since his kindness yielded no results he was going to throw them in jail until they confessed their lies.

The town jail cells were horrible places "dark, acrid with old and disreputable odors, full of harsh discordant echoes, and shut in by iron bars from the world of free men."[72] Most of the other occupants were not reputable characters, but rather petty criminals and drunkards. This was the cell chosen for the three children of Fatima. Opening the cell door, the Tinsmith threatened to boil the children in oil if they persisted in their refusal to divulge the Secret of Fatima. Still in their presence, he ordered that a cauldron of oil be heated, and threatened to put the children in the cauldron if they did not cooperate. He then left them in the cell to allow them time to ponder the situation.

The children immediately retreated to the back of the cell near the barred window that overlooked the cattle market. Jacinta peered out and began to cry telling Lucia, "…We are going to die without ever seeing our parents again. I want to see my mother!" Lucia tried to take Jacinta's mind off her mother by suggesting that the three children each take one of the intentions for which the Lady had asked them to pray – sinners, the Holy Father and reparation for the sins committed against the Immaculate Heart of Mary. Though agreeing, when asked to choose the one she preferred, Jacinta responded, "I'm

---

[72] Walsh, William Thomas, *Our Lady of Fatima*, Image Book, Doubleday Publishing, 1954. page 109.

making the offering for all the intentions, because I love them all." "With her face bathed in tears, she joined her hands, raised her eyes to heaven and said, 'O my Jesus! This is for love of You, for the conversion of sinners, for the Holy Father, and in reparation for the sins committed against the Immaculate Heart of Mary!'"

Soon thereafter, Jacinta's thoughts would again drift to her mother. This time it was Francisco who reminded her "If we never see our mother again, patience! Let us offer it for the conversion of sinners. The worst will be if Our Lady never comes back any more. That's what bothers me. But I am going to offer that, too, for the conversion of sinners."

This gentle reminder was enough to satisfy Jacinta for a while though similar conversations occurred many times throughout the ordeal often resulting in the three children kneeling in prayer in the cell amidst the adult prisoners.

Such a prison spectacle obviously attracted the attention of the other prisoners who gathered around the children with their questions. One of the imprisoned men tried to persuade Jacinta to give in, telling her that she could avoid being killed by simply telling the secret to the Administrator, but Jacinta responded, "I'd rather die!" Jacinta then rose from her kneeling position, removed the medal containing an image of Our Lady from her neck, and asked a tall prisoner to hang it on a nail that was in the wall. She immediately knelt again. The prisoners also got on their knees and joined the children in prayer saying only the prayers that they knew. When the Rosary ended, Jacinta went back to the window and began to cry again. Despite offering the sacrifice to Jesus, she was still saddened thinking about her mother.

One of the prisoners who developed a fondness for little Jacinta decided to play the concertina to divert the child's attention from her plight. As he played, they all started singing, children and adults together. One of the prisoners asked if the children knew how to dance to which they replied, "Yes. We know the Fandango and the Vira; two folk dances that are very popular in Fatima region of Portugal particularly during celebrations such as those held in commemoration of a Saint. And, there was no shortage of such celebrations in a country as religious as Portugal. In fact, each region popularized its own style of dance for that purpose, dance styles such as the Vira, Chula, Corridinho, Malhao and Fandango. The Vira, very popular in the Fatima region, is similar to the Australian Waltz, where couples form a circle facing each-other and go around a circle doing different steps, changing partners as they go, although sometimes the women have solo parts. Typically, these dances are performed in costume consisting of a long length red and black skirt with a flower pattern on the hem of the skirt. Women wear a white shirt and a red head-piece. The Fandango is like the Vira, in the steps, but the music is much different. Originally formed in Spain, this dance is much loved and celebrated in Portugal not only on special saint celebrations but also at Christmas. The traditional costume of the Fandango is a long red skirt and a red shirt.

Today, however, there would be no costume, nor would there be any precept of a formal celebration. Rather the entire ruse was simply a distraction by a kindly cellmate from the horror that this moment presented to the children. The poor thief sharing Jacinta's cell tried to dance with her but found her to be so tiny that he was forced to pick her up and dance with her in his arms.

Lucia knew how much Jacinta loved to dance and recalled that she was quite good at it. In her mind's eye, Lucia drifted back to the day that Jacinta learned that one of her brothers was killed in the war, recalling how much she cried. Even then, Lucia could distract her, by arranging a little dance with two of her other brothers. There was the poor child dancing away as she dried the tears that ran down her cheeks. Her fondness for dancing was such, that the sound of some shepherd playing his instrument in the pasture was enough to start her dancing all by herself.[73]

At least for the time being, as they danced to the sounds of the concertina, the children didn't think so much about the boiling caldron of oil that awaited them. The music and dancing stopped abruptly, however, when a policeman entered the cell and summoned the children to follow him to the office of the Administrator.

The Tinsmith made another attempt to extract the secret from the children who met his demand with an unambiguous silence. "Very well," the frustrated official said, "I have tried to save you. But since you will not obey the government, you shall be boiled alive in a cauldron of hot oil."[74] He shouted a

---

[73] Dos Santos, Sr. Lucia, Fatima in Lucia's Own Words. The Remembrances of Sister Lucia, 20th Edition, 2016. pages 52-54 and 92-93. Also, http://www.theholy-rosary.org/fatimaapparitions.

[74] Walsh, William Thomas, Our Lady of Fatima, Image Book, Doubleday Publishing, 1954. page 113.

command and the door to his office opened. On the other side stood a very big guard with a contemptuous look on his face. "Is the oil good and hot?" the Administrator inquired of him. "Yes, Senhor Administrator," came the reply. "Boiling," the Administrator demanded. "Yes Senhor," the guard insisted. Grabbing Jacinta by the arm, the Administrator instructed, "Take this one and throw her in."

Francisco and Lucia were certain she had gone to her death and began to pray for her courage. "What do we care if they kill us? Francisco offered. "We'll go right to heaven." Soon the door reopened and the ugly guard said, "She's fried, now for the next one." He grabbed Francisco and pulled him out of the room slamming the door behind him.

Lucia was now alone with the Administrator. "It will be you next," he said. "You'd better tell me the secret, Lucia." With marked indifference Lucia replied, "I would rather die." "Very well. You shall," the Administrator obliged. The Administrator was certainly aware of the political problems the torturous death of such innocent children would bring, however, and had no plans to do anything beyond scaring the three innocents into confessing.

Shortly thereafter the guard returned, grabbed Lucia's arm and led her away to another room where Lucia was delighted to see Francisco and Jacinta alive.

Administrator de Oliveira Santos was defeated. He kept the children overnight perhaps still holding out hope that they might relent, but was forced to release them the following morning.[75]

WEDNESDAY AUGUST 15, 1917
THE FEAST OF THE ASSUMPTION OF MARY

Olimpia and Manuel Marto attended morning Mass at the Church of St. Anthony. They prayed for guidance and grieved for the loss of their children at the hands of the Administrator. Nearly everyone at church that morning spoke of the kidnapping and rumors that the children had been transferred and were now incarcerated at Santarem, a larger, more penal-type facility. One reported that they were

---

[75]Ibid, page 112-113. Also, http://www.fatima.org/essentials/opposed/seerkidn.asp.

seen playing on the porch of the Administrator's house in Ourem. Another said they were on the porch at the rectory in Fatima, a rumor which in fact proved to be true. Marto grabbed his daughter in his arms and sobbed as he held on to her tightly. The crowd that lingered after Mass was visibly overjoyed but at the same time clenched fists and shared some very angry words toward the Administrator. Marto spoke to the crowd urging them to behave as the problem was not with any individual but rather with the unbelief that persisted from those in control.

Just then, the Administrator, who had taken the children back to the rectory, approached. He asked Marto to join him in a glass of wine, an offer that Marto very quickly rejected. The crowd, however, grew angrier and, if not for the intervention of Manuel Marto, the Tinsmith may well have been injured at the hand of the angry mob. As the enraged horde moved toward the Tinsmith, Marto quickly changed his mind and agreed to accept the Administrator's offer to have a glass of wine at the nearby shop.

While all this was developing, the children quietly slipped away and headed for the Cova where they recited the Rosary at the foot of the small holm oak upon which Our Lady had appeared to them. The tree now stood almost devoid of its foliage and even missed a few branches that pilgrims had carried away as souvenirs. The children also took notice of the arch and table left by Maria Carreira on August 13th. On it lay some flowers and two candlesticks that pilgrims had left as homage. Maria Carreira had already gathered several coins that had been left there as well. In all there were 1340 reis – just under 2 US dollars.

The morning return home after two days in captivity was certainly cause for happiness and Jacinta and Francisco's parents wanted their children to remain at home with them so they could properly celebrate their return. To relieve Francisco and Jacinta of their chore Manuel and Olympia Marto sent their son John out to pasture the sheep instead.[76]

Lucia, on the other hand, received no such warm welcome and upon her return home was immediately instructed to get the sheep and take them to the pasture, a request to which she obediently complied.[77]

---

[76] John Marto died April 28, 2000.
[77] Dos Santos, Sr. Lucia, Fatima in Lucia's Own Words. The Remembrances of Sister Lucia, 20th Edition, 2016. Page 92. Also, http://www.fatima.org/essentials/opposed/seerkidn.asp.

AUGUST 16, 1917 – AUGUST 18, 1917

Over the course of the ensuing three days the children pastured their sheep as normal, each day hoping for an appearance by the Lady. At the end of each day they returned home in disappointment for lack of an appearance.

SUNDAY AUGUST 19, 1917
MORNING

Sunday August 19th was clear, sunny and typically hot when Maria Carreira awoke. Up until now, she was unable to convince anyone to take charge of the money that she had collected at the Cova da Iria. On this day, however, she awoke earlier than most days to allow time to search out Lucia in the hope of convincing her, if not to take the money, to at least ask Our Lady what should be done with it. Finding Lucia, Maria made her plea, but Lucia steadfastly refused to accept responsibility for the cash. "At least," Maria begged, "ask Our Lady what should be done with the money that was collected."[78] To this request Lucia consented.

Lucia then went to meet Francisco and his brother John and together, they led the sheep to pasture on the Serra. For reasons that are unclear, Jacinta did not pasture the sheep this day. During the course of the day the three "children strolled, played, talked and said their prayers" all while keeping a watchful eye on their flock

By late afternoon the children, with their sheep, had wandered to a hollow in the rocks called Valinhos. They lingered about midway between Aljustrel and the cave on the northern slope of Cabeco.

---

[78] Walsh, William Thomas, Our Lady of Fatima, Image Book, Doubleday Publishing, 1954, page 119.

APPROXIMATELY 4:00 IN THE AFTERNOON

While at Cabeco, Lucia sensed a subtle change in the atmosphere, it was a feeling similar to the way things always felt before a supernatural visitation. Francisco felt it too and they knew that the Lady was about to appear. It suddenly dawned on Lucia that Jacinta was not with them and she pleaded with John to quickly run to get her, that she might not miss the vision. Francisco too begged his brother who steadfastly refused to leave, that is until Lucia offered to pay him two vintens, small coins valued at about a penny each, for his trouble. Then he quickly ran off to fetch his sister. Several minutes passed and Francisco and Lucia saw the usual flash of light just about the same time that they noticed Jacinta running toward them.

A moment later, the Lady appeared atop a holm-oak tree, not unlike the one at the Cova, and the children fell to their knees. Our Lady looked at them tenderly as if to console them for their suffering. "What is it that you want of me?" Lucia asked as she had in all the previous apparitions. *"I want you to continue going to the Cova da Iria on the 13th, and to continue praying the Rosary every day. In the last month, I will perform a miracle so that all may believe."* Remembering her promise to Maria, Lucia asked, "What do you want done with the money that the people leave in the Cova da Iria?" *"Have two pedestals made,"* the Lady replied. *"One is to be carried by you and Jacinta and two other girls dressed in white; the other one is to be carried by Francisco and three other boys. The money from the pedestals is for the 'festa' of Our Lady of the Rosary, and what is left over will help towards the construction of a chapel that is to be built here."* As she had in the past, Lucia asked the Lady if she would cure some of the sick that had made the request of her. *"Yes,"* the Lady responded, *"I will cure some of them during the year."* Then, looking very sad, Our Lady said, *"Pray, pray very much, and make sacrifices for sinners; for many souls go to hell, because there are none to sacrifice themselves and to pray for them."* As she finished this admonishment she ascended towards the east as she had in the previous apparitions.[79] For a long time the children remained kneeling in their typical post-visit state of ecstasy. When they

---

[79] Dos Santos, Sr. Lucia, Fatima in Lucia's Own Words. The Remembrances of Sister Lucia, 20th Edition, 2016. Page 92. Also, Walsh, William Thomas, Our Lady of Fatima,

were finally able to move, Jacinta "cut off some branches of the shrub on which the Lady had stood, and took them home."[80] She gave some of them to her father who examined them remarking at the beautiful fragrance they emitted. Then the children went to Lucia's house and Jacinta presented some of the branches to Maria Rosa saying, "O Aunt, our Lady has appeared again' These are the places where She put Her feet." Maria Rosa responded, "I thought the administrator had finished with all that, and here you are still telling lies. I know what you need."[81] Yet later, after smelling the branch, Maria Rosa noticed that there was something "singularly sweet" in the fragrance that had gone unnoticed when Jacinta first presented it.

This marked the fourth time that Our Lady appeared to the three children. This time, however, Lucia believed strongly that the suggestion of sacrifice spoken of by the Lady was to include the practice of mortification.[82]

THE DAYS FOLLOWING AUGUST 19, 1917

Some days later, as the children led their sheep to pasture, Lucia found a thick piece of rope on a narrow street of Aljustrel. She picked it up and tied it around her arm for fun, but noticed that before long, it began to hurt. It was then that she suggested to her cousins that they tie it around their waists, against their bare skin, as a sacrifice to God. They both agreed and, laying the rope against a rock, they used a sharp-edged stone like a knife, to divide the rope into three pieces. The rope was very rough and wearing it on their waists caused a great deal of pain, so much so, that Jacinta would sometimes cry because of it. Whenever this happened, Lucia would suggest that she remove the rope, but

---

Image Book, Doubleday Publishing, 1954. pages 119-120. Also, http://www.theholy-rosary.org/fatimaapparitions.

[80] Walsh, William Thomas, Our Lady of Fatima, Image Book, Doubleday Publishing, 1954 page 121.

[81] McGlynn, Fr. Thomas, O.P., Vision of Fatima, Washington, DC, 1948. page 48. Also, Walsh, William Thomas, Our Lady of Fatima, Image Book, Doubleday Publishing, 1954. page 121.

[82] Dos Santos, Sr. Lucia, Fatima in Lucia's Own Words. The Remembrances of Sister Lucia, 20th Edition, 2016. page 92-93.

Jacinta would reply, "No! I want to offer this sacrifice to Our Lord in reparation, and for the conversion of sinners."[83] This was the children's first experiment with mortification, but it would not be their last.

On another day, while at play, the children picked plants off the walls and pressed them in their hands to "hear them crack." While plucking the plants, Jacinta grabbed a bunch of nettles receiving a painful sting. Stinging nettles, a plant indigenous to the Fatima region of Portugal, have developed stinging cells as an adaptation to deter herbivores from eating them. The plants contain long, thin, hollow hairs that cover much of the stem and the underside of the leaves. Nettle stings contain formic acid, histamine and other chemicals that inflict a painful sting when touched. As soon as she felt the pain she squeezed them even more tightly in her hands saying, "Look! Look! Here is something else with which we can mortify ourselves!" The children took her suggestion and from time to time would hit their legs with nettles as an offering of sacrifice to God.

Jacinta was very serious about making sacrifices as instructed by Our Lady and never allowed a single opportunity to pass her by. There were two poor families in Moita whose children would beg for food door to door. The three seers met them one day as they walked with the sheep. Jacinta immediately suggested, "Let's give our lunch to those poor children, for the conversion of sinners." "And she ran to take it to them"[84]

From that moment, the three agreed that anytime they met any poor children they would relinquish their lunches to them. Before long, the children would take great care to be sure they met the three visionaries by waiting for them along the road. As soon as the poor children were spotted, Jacinta would run to give them the lunches. Doing this, and the thought of sacrifice, made her very happy. On these days, the three seers "ate only pine nuts and little berries about the size of an olive, which grow on the roots of yellow bell-flowers, as well as blackberries, mushrooms, and some other things" that could be found on the roots of pine trees.[85]

But on this day, later that afternoon, Jacinta told Lucia she was hungry. There were both holm-oak and oak trees nearby that bore acorns, but they were

---

[83] Ibid, page 93.
[84] Ibid, page 46-47.
[85] Ibid, pages 47 and 93.

still green. Despite their early stage of growth, Lucia said they were edible. Francisco climbed the holm-oaks, picking the acorns until his pockets were full. But before eating, Jacinta remembered that the acorns from the oak trees were more bitter than those of the holm-oak and decided to eat only those, offering it as a sacrifice. This became one of her usual sacrifices, often picking the acorns off the oaks or the unripened olives from the olive trees. One day, Lucia warned Jacinta that they were too bitter, but Jacinta said, "But it's because it's bitter that I'm eating it, for the conversion of sinners."[86]

One very hot August day a neighbor offered Lucia's mother a good pasture for their sheep. Though a long distance, it is an area that has shade trees and a pond nearby where the flocks would be able to drink. Maria Rosa instructed Lucia to take siesta beneath a tree where the shade would offer protection from the sun. On the way, Lucia and her cousins met the poor children and Jacinta ran to give them their food before continuing their journey. Though a lovely day the sun was blazing. It seemed that, in that arid and stony wasteland over which they walked, the sun might just burn everything up.

Naturally, the three cousins became very thirsty. Jacinta had an insatiable thirst, but there was nothing to drink along the way. They offered their thirst as a sacrifice initially, but by mid-afternoon, they were compelled to walk to a nearby house and asked a little old lady who lived there for some water. The woman gave Lucia a pitcher of water and some bread which Lucia accepted and promptly offered to share with Jacinta and Francisco. Both refused to partake, however, as a sacrifice for the conversion of sinners. Feeling guilty for her lack of restrain, Lucia poured the contents of the pitcher into a hallow in a rock so the sheep could drink it instead. Lucia then returned the pitcher to the old woman.

As the day got even hotter, they could hear the crickets and frogs from the pond making quite a racket. Jacinta asked Lucia to "tell the crickets and the frogs to keep quiet! I have such a terrible headache." Lucia knew that Jacinta's ailment was from her hunger and thirst. It was then that Francisco reminded Jacinta that she could offer the headache and the noise as a sacrifice for the conversion of sinners. Jacinta clasped her "head between her two little hands, saying, 'Yes, I do. Let them sing!'"

---

[86] Ibid, page 47.

It was clear that the children's sacrifices were pleasing to God but even Lucia noticed something special about the penances made by Jacinta. She had become a different person; no longer the whiney, belligerent type that always insisted on getting her way, but a more "patient, more long-suffering, more affectionate" person who seemed to have been "infused with the gift of wisdom."[87] Lucia even noticed objective signs of some miracles that she attributed to Jacinta's intervention. There was, for example, the wretched woman with a terrible disease that the children happened upon one day. Moved by her condition, Jacinta said three Aves for the woman and all her symptoms left her. Another woman in Aljustrel constantly ridiculed the three children following their apparitions. She called them liars and imposters which greatly bothered the children, but after Jacinta prayed for the woman's conversion, she never again spoke an unkind word to them.

It was also in August that Lucia noticed that her mother "began to feel a little more at peace" with the possibility of the apparitions. Maria Rosa would say, "If there were even just one more person who had seen something, why then, I might believe! But among all these people, they're [the children] the only ones who saw anything!" But even as more and more people began reporting visions of Our Lady or various signs in the sun, etc., Maria Rosa declared, "I used to think before, that if there were just one other person who saw anything, then I'd believe; but now, so many people say they have seen something, and I still don't believe!" Around that same time, Lucia's father also began to defend her and to silence Lucia's critics saying, "We don't know if it's true, but neither do we know if it's a lie."[88]

Just as Lucia's parents were finally showing a bit more sympathy for their daughter, the Martos were losing their patience. Olimpia complained of having to continually send someone to fetch her children, simply to please the people who came asking to speak with them. She therefore handed over the care of the flock to her other son John enabling Jacinta and Francisco to remain near the house. This decision caused Jacinta great pain for two reasons: first,

---

[87] Walsh, William Thomas, Our Lady of Fatima, Image Book, Doubleday Publishing 1954

[88] Dos Santos, Sr. Lucia, Fatima in Lucia's Own Words. The Remembrances of Sister Lucia, 20th Edition, 2016. page 93-94.

because she was now forced to speak to everyone who came looking for her and, second, because she was no longer able to spend the whole day with Lucia. But Olimpia offered Jacinta no alternative.

To escape from the unwelcome visitors, she and Francisco would hide in Loca do Cabeco, the cave hallowed out in the rock on the slope of the hill of Cabeco on top of which stood a windmill. Situated as it is on the eastern slope facing their hamlet, this hiding place is so well formed that it afforded them an ideal protection from both the rain and the burning sun, especially since it is sheltered by many oak and olive trees. How many were the prayers and sacrifices that Jacinta offered there to Jesus! Flowers of innumerable varieties grew all over the slope. Among them were many irises for which Jacinta had a special love. Every evening Jacinta would wait for Lucia to walk past on her way home, holding an iris she had picked for her, or some other flower if there were no irises to be found. Jacinta took great joy in plucking off the petals one by one strewing them over Lucia.

Like Olimpia, Maria Rosa too was weary of the throngs of people requesting an audience with Lucia, but was satisfied for the time being with deciding each day where Lucia was to pasture the sheep, so that she knew where to find her when she was needed. When the place was nearby, Lucia would tell her little cousins who lost no time in coming out to join her. Jacinta would run until she caught sight of Lucia. Then, exhausted, would sit down and keep calling to her until Lucia answered and ran to meet her. Eventually though, Maria Rosa could no longer accept wasting her other daughter's time going to replace Lucia in the pasture every time a stranger would ask to speak to her and she decided to sell the lot.

She talked things over with Olimpia and the two agreed to send the children off to school. At playtime during school hours, Jacinta loved to make a visit to the Blessed Sacrament. But even there, crowds of people would find them. "They seem to guess," Jacinta would tell Lucia, "We are no sooner inside the church than a crowd of people come asking us questions! I wanted so much to be alone for a long time with the Hidden Jesus and talk to Him, but they never let us." It was true, the simple country folk never left them alone. With the utmost simplicity, they told the children all about their needs, their troubles, their ailments. Jacinta showed the greatest compassion, especially when it concerned some sinner, saying 'We must pray and offer sacrifices to Our Lord, so that he will be converted and not go to hell, poor man!'[89]

WEDNESDAY SEPTEMBER 12, 1917

On the day prior to the next highly anticipated appearance of Our Lady, pilgrims from all corners of the hill country jammed the streets. By nightfall, the strangers, faithful, naysayers, and curiosity seekers alike, also crowded the yard surrounding the two homes of the three visionaries. Many slept in the fields so that by sunrise on the following day, they could make their way to Cova da Iria to view the promised appearance of the Lady.

THURSDAY SEPTEMBER 13, 1917

Morning found many in the crowd saying the Rosary. The multitude by now was an estimated 30,000 strong and they crammed the roads and fields from Aljustrel to Fatima. As the hour approached, Lucia, Jacinta and Francisco set out to the Cova but had great difficulty navigating the mass of people. Everyone wanted to see the children and speak with them in advance of the Lady's appearance. Showing no respect for the others, simple folk struggled to break through the crowd that pressed around the children. As soon as someone reached one of the children, he would throw himself to his knees and beg to have his petition presented to the Lady. Those who couldn't get close enough shouted from a distance. "For the love of God, ask Our Lady to cure my son who is a cripple," one would cry. "And to cure mine who is blind," another would say. "To cure mine who is deaf!...To bring back my husband, son, who has gone to war! ...To convert sinners! ...To give me back my health as I have

---

[89] Dos Santos, Sr. Lucia, Fatima in Lucia's Own Words. The Remembrances of Sister Lucia, 20th Edition, 2016. pages 54-55.

tuberculosis!..." On and on it went so as to make it seem that all the afflictions of poor humanity were assembled there. Some even climbed to the tops of the trees and still others, walls, just for the opportunity to see the children pass.[90] The scene reminded Lucia of Jesus's passage through Palestine, as it was utter chaos and the children were victims of the mayhem. The children responded yes to some of the petitioners and offered a hand to others helping them rise from the dusty ground. And they managed to inch forward, mostly because of some kindly gentlemen that walked ahead of them opening a passage through which the children could pass the multitude. Lucia thought about the faithful people of Portugal. If they would do all this to humble themselves before "three poor children just because they were mercifully granted the grace to speak to [who many believed was] the Mother of God, what would they not do if they saw Our Lord Himself in person before them?" She was grateful for the extraordinary faith of these people. On this day, some thirty young seminarians and five or six priests joined the crowd of onlookers. Among the priests were the Reverend Monsignor Joao Quaresm, the Reverend Father Manuel Pereira da Silva, then a curate at Leiria, the Prior of Santa Catalina and Monsignor Manuel do Carmo Gois. The four left Leiria in a horse-drawn carriage early that morning to be on hand to witness the apparition. It seems that Reverend da Silva was more curious than faithful but endured the long, arduous journey regardless. They secured a place on some high ground overlooking the "vast natural amphitheater, already dark and seething with human forms."[91]

APPROXIMATELY 12:00 NOON

The children, with thousands of people in tow, finally reached the Cova da Iria only to find thousands more already assembled there. The silence was almost eerie as the children knelt before the holm-oak tree and began to say the Rosary. Many of the thirty thousand joined them in chorus. Suddenly people began to shout out with rejoice, praising Our Lady. Some pointed high above

---

[90] Ibid, page 181.
[91] Walsh, William Thomas, Our Lady of Fatima, Image Book, Doubleday Publishing, 1954. page 126.

prompting others to look in that direction. Monsignor Joao also noticed some-one pointing and looked up to observe "a luminous globe that moved from the east toward the west, slowly and majestically gliding down across the distance."[92] His friend saw the globe too as it moved westward, but just as suddenly as it appeared, it vanished, right before their eyes. Looking toward his friend Monsignor Joao said, "What do you think of that globe?" He answered with some enthusiasm and without hesitation, "That it was Our Lady."[93]

On this they agreed! Unlike them, and many of the thousands of on-lookers who could see only the light that carried her to the holm-oak tree, however, the shepherd children were privileged to look directly upon the face of the Mother of God, though the lady still had not yet identified herself to the children as such.

The children were once again engaged in conversation with Our Lady though this, the conversation in the fifth apparition of Our Lady to the children, would be the shortest of all. *"Continue to pray the Rosary in order to obtain the end of the war,"* the Lady said. *"In October Our Lord will come, as well as Our Lady of Sorrows and Our Lady of Mount Carmel. Saint Joseph will appear with the Child Jesus to bless the world. God is pleased with your sacrifices. He does not want you to sleep with the rope on, but only to wear it during the daytime."*[94] "I was told to ask you many things, the cure of some sick people, of a deaf-mute...," Lucia said. The Lady replied, *"Yes, I will cure some, but not others. In October, I will perform a miracle so that all may believe."* With that, Our Lady rose as usual and disappeared to the east.[95] The length of the apparition didn't matter to the children so long as they got to see her face once again, and this visit brought the promise that in October, the children would also look upon the face of Jesus.

---

[92] Walsh, William Thomas, Our Lady of Fatima, Image Book, Doubleday Publishing, 1954.page 126-127.

[93] Walsh, William Thomas, Our Lady of Fatima, Image Book, Doubleday Publishing, 1954. page 127.

[94] Dos Santos, Sr. Lucia, Fatima in Lucia's Own Words. The Remembrances of Sister Lucia, 20th Edition, 2016. page 181.

[95] Ibid, page 181-182. Also, http://www.theholyrosary.org/fatimaapparitions.

THURSDAY SEPTEMBER 29, 1917

Unbeknownst to most of the 30,000 onlookers attending the September 13th apparition the Reverend Doctor Manuel Nunes Formigao, who served as the cannon of the cathedral of Lisboa and a professor at the Seminary of Santarem was present that day. This learned man of integrity was asked by the Administrator of the Patriarchate in Lisboa to attend the apparition and report his findings to the government; findings that the Administrator quite assuredly assumed would debunk the myth of the apparitions. Though Formigao was not one of the chosen who was able to see the luminous globe, he interviewed enough people who did see it that he found it necessary to explore the phenomenon in more detail. On this day, he returned to Aljustrel to question some of those involved. He began by meeting with Maria Rosa dos Santos and Olimpia Marta who immediately sent for the children. Jacinta was first to arrive home and seemed a bit intimidated by the stranger. Though more emboldened when Francisco arrived, Formigao decided to depose Francisco first and sent Jacinta out to play. Francisco answered the questions posed to him with calmness and certainty. The Doctor then recalled Jacinta for questioning. Lucia arrived last and she too was questioned by Formigao. Hers was without a doubt the longest and most intense questioning. He tried to have her admit that she had apparitions of Our Lady prior to May 1917. Perhaps confusing it with rumors he may have heard about the apparitions she had of the Angel of Peace the year prior, but she would not be tripped up. He also tried to convince Lucia to reveal the secrets given the children by Our Lady but Lucia refused to divulge any such information.

Certainly, there were some minor differences in the accounts provided by the three children, such as whether Our Lady had on a pair of earrings, but no discrepancies of any real significance. Fr. Formigao ended his interrogation of the three children and returned to the Seminary of Santarem to evaluate the information he collected. His overall impression of the children was favorable, but perhaps, he thought, he could garner more information with a second round of precisely worded questions that might expose any deceits or satanic agencies.

MONDAY OCTOBER 10, 1917
11:00 PM

To that end, Formigao boarded a train for Chao da Macas eleven days later where he hired a horse and buggy to take him to Vila Nova de Ourem. It was 11:00 PM when he reached his destination in Montelo, two miles outside of Fatima. There, under the pen name of "the Visconde de Montelo," he lodged with a family that was able to tell him all about the Marto and dos Santos families. He learned that the families were not poor but did nothing to capitalize on the apparitions and in fact had tried to discourage people from gathering on their land. While Manuel dos Santos would drink a bit more than he perhaps should, Maria Rosa was an honest, devout woman with an incredible work ethic. Similarly, Antonio Marto was incapable of deceit, and both he and Olimpia had a deep faith and practiced their Catholic religion always. The children were equally well liked and though most people disbelieved them in May and June, most were now "inclined to accept their story, since so many had seen the cloud over the tree on August 13th and had noted the other strange phenomena in August and September."[96] Formigao had gotten all the information he needed and it was now time to confront the children once again.

TUESDAY OCTOBER 11, 1917

Tuesday found Formigao back at the home of Antonio dos Santos. While they waited for Lucia to arrive, Formigao asked Maria Rosa if she had ever told Lucia the story of the Apparitions of Our Lady to the two shepherd children at the southern France village of LaSalette wondering aloud if she may have been influenced by this story. Though these Apparitions took place over 70 years prior, there were many similarities; the two most striking being that Our Lady told secrets to the children which were revealed only to Pius IX, and She offered warnings of coming calamities if the good people of France didn't

---

[96] Walsh, William Thomas, Our Lady of Fatima, Image Book, Doubleday Publishing, 1954. page 132-133.

stop offending God. Maria Rosa, though admitting to telling the story, thought it a non-factor for Lucia, noting that her daughter never mentioned the story again.

Lucia finally arrived home and Formigao questioned her in the presence of four witnesses about minute details of the Apparitions. Did Our Lady ever finger the Rosary Beads? (No.) What Did the Lady promise to do to get the crowd to believe she had appeared? (She said She would perform a miracle.) And how many times did she mention it? (A few times, once at the first Apparition and when I asked her the question.) Are you afraid the crowd will harm you if there is no miracle? (I haven't any fear.) Did she tell you to pray for the conversion of sinners? (No. She told me to pray to the Lady of the Rosary so that the war would end. She asked for sacrifices rather than prayers for the conversion of sinners.) The questioning continued in this fashion until Formigao was satisfied. Then he turned his attention to Jacinta for re-examination, and then to Francisco. The line of questioning for the latter two was the same as with Lucia. At the end of this tedious process, Dr. Formigao was convinced that all three children had told the truth and felt that the final test of their veracity would be the miracle promised for the October 13th Apparition. That is an appointment he vowed not to miss.

WEDNESDAY OCTOBER 12, 1917

Around this same time, Fr. Pocas, Prior of Porto de Mos, also examined the children. He was not nearly as professional or courteous as Dr. Formigeo, however, and treated the children with animosity and contempt. "Look here, girl," he said to Lucia, "now you are going to tell me that all this is lies and witchcraft. If you don't say so, I will say it and have it said everywhere... Everybody will believe me... and you shall not escape!" Much to his chagrin, Lucia remained silent. Despite his tactics, at the end, he too admitted that he thought the children had told the truth.

As the big day approached, Maria Rosa was convinced that the day's events would expose Lucia as a fraud and she feared for her daughter's safety. The fear was not experienced by Maria Rosa alone however. Lucia's entire family panicked as October 13, 1917 drew near. Lucia could not escape her promise, they thought. It was far too specific. A miracle for the whole world to see on Saturday October 13, 1917 at 12:00 Noon. Everyone would know immediately when the miracle does not happen and the crowd of so many will be angry. Only God knows what the consequences will be!

Maria Rosa tried one final time to reason with Lucia. Please, "it's better for us to go and tell everything. People say we are going to die tomorrow in the Cova da Iria. If the Lady does not make the miracle, the crowd will kill us," she pleaded. "I am not afraid, Mother," Lucia answered calmly. "I am sure the Lady will do everything she has promised." Maria Rosa suggested they go to confession so they will be prepared for death. Lucia agreed to go but not for the reason her mother conceived.

Outside it was cool and breezy. A light mist had begun to fall and it was clear that a storm was approaching. It promised to be a long night as the drizzle turned to a hard, wind driven rain!

SATURDAY OCTOBER 13, 2017
MORNING

Since the last Apparition in September, word continued to spread through the entire region of Fatima and an area well beyond. Many of the thousands that waited with great anticipation for the Lady's final appearance on October 13, 1917 were devout Catholics. They would not be deterred by the torrential rains and gale winds that greeted Fatima's dawn and continued to pummel the area throughout the morning. Despite the gloomy weather, over 70,000 people lined the streets and waited in the trampled fields. Many were barefoot as they plodded through the mud of the Cova da Iria. All were soaked to the skin despite the many who tried to shield themselves from the wind-driven rain with umbrellas. Parents carried their children. Adults carried baskets of food and jugs of water over their shoulders. Others packed them on donkeys that they guided along the streets. Some were skeptical, other curious. Some hoped for a cure, some for forgiveness of their sins, others for material goods and still others for a simple blessing directly from the Mother of God.

Among the skeptics this day was Avelino de Almeida, the managing editor of *O Seculo*, the largest of the newspapers distributed in Lisboa. Almeida was a Freemason who volunteered for the assignment hoping to discredit the children's fable of a ghostly woman floating above a tree departing secrets to shepherds. He started his work the day before as he walked alongside other pilgrims taking mental notes of the experience which he would later reduce to writing for his newspaper.

The story that appeared in the Saturday paper of October 13, 1917 noted how he passed the barefooted men and women who

> *"carried their footgear in bags on their heads, the men leaning on great staves and carefully grasping umbrellas also. One would say they were all oblivious to what was going on about them, with a great lack of interest in the journey and in other travelers, as if lost in a dream, reciting their Rosary in a sad rhythmic chant. A woman says the first part of the Hail Mary; her companions in chorus say the second part of the prayer. With sure and rhythmical steps, they tread the dusty road which runs between the pine woods and the olive groves, so that they may arrive before night at the place of the apparition, where, under the serene and cold light of the stars, they hope they can sleep, keeping the first places near the blessed azinheira [holm-oak tree] so that today they can see better."*

Almeida did not portray himself as a radical Freemason intent on bringing about the demise of religion, but rather a non-believer who wished no harm, and did not intend to ridicule, those who believed. His story continued,

> *"Thousands of persons are hastening to a wild expanse of country near Ourem to see and hear the Virgin Mary. Let pious souls be not offended and pure believing hearts be not afraid; we have no intention of being a scandal for those who sincerely hold to their faith and whom the miraculous still attracts, seduces, bewitches, consoles and fortifies, as has been the case for thousands of years, and most certainly will be for other thousands of years! ...This is only a short newspaper article on an event which is not*

*new in the history of Catholicism. ....Some regard it as a message
from heaven and a grace; others see in it a sign and proof that
the spirit of superstition and fanaticism has planted deep roots
that it is difficult or even impossible to destroy.*

*Times of great calamities have always revived and renewed reli-
gious ideas and have favored them. And war, which strikes everywhere, offers them the most favorable and fertile soil for
growth. We see that confirmed in the life of the trenches and even
in the spiritual atmosphere of the belligerent countries. "*

After summarizing the events of Fatima from May to September, recounting
the previous Apparitions of Mary at Lourdes, La Sallette and other places, and pointing out the speculators who hoped to profit from such events, Almeida continued,

*"The miracle takes place between Noon and one o'clock, accord-
ing to those who have been there. But not all have the chance to
see the holy figure. The number of the elect seems very small. Despite their efforts, many see nothing. This is why those who find
themselves near the children are contented with hearing them
speak with an invisible partner. Others, on the contrary, see in a
divinely solemn moment the stars shining in the firmament, even
though the sun be at the zenith. They hear a subterranean groan-
ing which announces the presence of the Lady. They claim that the
temperature falls and they compare the impressions of that moment with those they have experienced during an eclipse of the
sun....*

*According to what the children say, the figure of the Virgin ap-
pears on an azinheira, surrounded on all sides by a nuage
[cloud].... The suggestion of the masses, brought there by the supernatural and captivated by a superhuman force, is so powerful
that eyes fill with tears, faces become as pale as corpses, men and
women throw themselves on their knees, chant songs and recite
the Rosary together.*

*We do not know if there have already been blind persons who have
recovered their sight, paralytics who have regained the use of their*

limbs, hardened sinners who are turned back from the straight ways of sin to plunge into the purifying water of penance.

But that matters little. The news of the apparitions has spread from Algarve to the Minho. Since the Day of the Ascension the pilgrims have flocked there by thousands on the thirteenth of each month, from near and far. The means of transportation do not suffice.

The clergy of the place and the neighborhood maintain, as regards the events, a prudent reserve, at least in appearance. It is the custom of the Church. It proclaims loudly that in such circumstances doubt means nothing, for doubts also come from the devil. But secretly it rejoices over the great concourse of pilgrims who since May have become more and more numerous.

And there are even people who dream of a great and magnificent church, always full, of large hotels nearby with every modern comfort, of shops well stocked with a thousand and one different objects of piety and souvenirs of Our Lady of Fatima, and of a railway which will take us to the future miraculous sanctuary with more convenience that he buses in which, for the moment, the mass of the faithful and of the curious now achieve this right.... '[97]

The Marto and dos Santos families, meanwhile were waking to the dreadful weather that awaited them. People, strangers began arriving early and continued to come throughout the morning. Many simply walked in, as if invited, tracking mud and dripping water on the floors inside. They asked to see the children. Just a word with them was all they needed. At the Marto house, some even went so far as to make themselves at home sitting on the chairs and the beds. "Get out of here, all of you!" Olimpia screamed to inattentive ears.[98]

Lucia and Jacinta declined offers of new ornate dresses from the Baroness from Pombalinho preferring instead to dress in their communion dresses. All the children managed some breakfast and then prepared to leave. Maria Rosa had no intention of going, but at the last minute grabbed her shawl, turned to Lucia and said through her tears, "I know they are going to kill you. Very well, then, if you must go, I will go and

---

[97] Walsh, William Thomas, Our Lady of Fatima, Image Book, Doubleday Publishing, 1954. page 139-141.
[98] Ibid, page 142

die with you."[99] While these may not have been words of comfort, they were likely the most supporting words that Maria Rosa had spoken to Lucia since May.

On October 13, 1917, a crowd estimated to be as large as 70,000 converged on the Cova da Iria, land owned by Lucia's parents, to witness the anticipated miracle that, according to the children, was promised by Our Lady. No one in the crowd was disappointed.

The roads along Fatima enroute to Cova da Iria were jammed with people, thousands of them, who kneeled in the mud as the children passed pleading with the children to carry their petitions to Our Lady. The crowds made the travel very slow and the pouring rain and mud-soaked streets made it appear even longer. As they approached the Cova, so many people, 70,000 in all, blocked the way. If not for one man who hoisted Jacinta up on his shoulders yelling "make way for the children who saw Our Lady," they may not have made it to the holm-oak tree. Manuel Marto followed close behind the man with Lucia, Francisco and Maria Rosa on either side of him. Upon reaching their destination, Manuel found Olimpia was already there waiting for them.

---

[99] Ibid.

Lucia's sister Maria stood at a distance, as her husband did not want her to go down the slope with the baby because the entire slope and Cova were covered with people.

Many continued to pray the Rosary as others scanned the sky through the rain looking for a sign of the Lady's arrival. A priest who arrived the night before was kneeling in the mud. He had been praying throughout the night and was now reading from his breviary. He turned to Lucia asking the time of Our Lady's arrival. "At midday," she responded. Then, as if moved by an interior impulse she yelled, "Put down your umbrellas" Though the rain still came down in torrents, some complied. "Put down your umbrellas." she repeated, as more began to heed her instruction.

APPROXIMATELY NOON

This photo was taken during the Miracle of the Sun on October 13, 1917 as the sun danced in the sky. Some looked up in amazement, others looked away in fear. Still others fell to their knees in prayer, but all 70,000 were witness to the miracle that Our Lady performed that day.

The priest, meanwhile, was growing impatient. "It's past midday," he said to Lucia, "Away with all this! It is all an illusion." He pushed the children along as if instructing them to depart, but they refused to be deterred. "Whoever wants to go, can go," Lucia said, "but I'm not going. Our Lady told us to come. We saw her other times and we're going to see her now." As the disappointment began to spread through the crowd, Lucia yelled, "Jacinta, kneel down, for now I see Our Lady there. I can see the flash!" Maria Rosa turned to Lucia and said, "Watch out, daughter! Don't let yourself be deceived!"[100] Her warning fell on deaf ears, as Lucia, "whose face had become flushed and transparently beautiful" was now staring into the face of Our Lady and had already become entranced in a state of ecstasy. Likewise, Jacinta and Francisco were also oblivious to the mass of people behind them as they stared upward, not at all bothered by the steady rain that pelted them. "What do you want of me?" Lucia asked as she had so many times before. Our Lady answered, *"I want to tell you that a chapel is to be built here in my honor. I am the Lady of the Rosary. Continue always to pray the Rosary every day. The war is going to end, and the soldiers will soon return to their homes."* "I have many things to ask you; the cure of some sick persons, the conversion of sinners…" Lucia continued listing some of the petitions brought to her from the crowds. As She had in the past, Our Lady verified that some petitions would be granted while others would not be granted, adding, *"They must amend their lives and ask forgiveness for their sins."* Then, with a very sad expression, She continued, *"Do not offend the Lord our God anymore because He is already so much offended."* When She finished speaking She opened her hands launching a ray of light in the direction of the sun.

APPROXIMATELY 12:30 PM TO 3:00 PM

As She ascended, the reflection of her own light continued to be projected on the sun itself. Lucia sensed this to be the promised sign and cried out to the crowd in a loud voice, "Look at the sun!" Suddenly the rain stopped, the clouds that previously covered the sun dissipated, and the sun appeared in the sky. Though exceptionally bright, the sun was not dazzling. Without warning, it began to turn in the sky as if projecting in each direction bands of light of each color that lit and colored the remaining clouds, the sky, the trees, and the crowd. It stayed for some moments then it went back to its normal position where it remained still for another short while.

---

[100] Ibid, page 144

As the 70,000 gazed upon the sky and, in particular, the sun, the children remained focused on the Lady of the Rosary, whose vision, though ascended, was now instantly replaced with a vision of St. Joseph holding the Child Jesus. Next to St. Joseph and standing beside the sun was Our Lady, this time wearing a white robe with a blue mantle. St. Joseph appeared to have blessed the world tracing the sign of the cross with his hand three times. As he did this Lucia said, "St. Joseph is going to bless us!" The Child Jesus did the same. All three children saw this vision while the next two were seen by Lucia alone. In the second vision "Our Lady of Sorrows in the somber garb assigned to her by tradition, the Mater Dolorosa of Good Friday, but without the sword in her breast, and beside her stood her divine Son, grieving as when he met her on the way to Calvary. Lucia saw only the upper part of His figure. He looked pityingly on the crowd for whom He had died, and raised His hand to make the sign of the cross over them."

In the third vision, Our Lady appeared as Our Lady of Mount Carmel. The Queen of heaven and earth held the baby Jesus upon Her knee.

A few in the crowd claimed to have seen the vision as well yet this claim remains unverified. No one else was privileged with such visions.

The entire mass, however, all 70,000 people, became aware that their clothes, as well as the ground beneath them, were completely dry. In amazement and confusion, they prayed, but just as suddenly as before, the sun looked as if it stood out from the sky appearing to fall on the now terrified crowd below. Most of the assembled fell to their knees and begged mercy. Though still intensely bright, people could look directly at the sun without hurting their eyes. As the crowd gazed at the burning orb, it seemed to "dance," then whirled like a giant wheel of fire. It did this for some time before stopping; then it quickly rotated again. Then brilliant colors began to reach down to the earth making all that could be seen tinted by the spectrum of colors. No one knew what to make of this and many continued to stare in utter amazement when, in an instant, the "fiery orb seemed to tremble, to shudder, and then to plunge precipitately, in a mighty zigzag, toward the crowd."[101] Many observers thought this was the end of the world. Terrified cries were heard from the crowd as some knelt in prayer and others ran for cover. Many critics of the children's "fantasies" were now

---

[101] Ibid, page 146.

believers who fell prostrate to the ground. The Marques do Cruz was heard to say, "Oh my God, how great is Thy power!"[102]

After about ten minutes the sun began to return to its rightful position in the sky following the same circuitous zigzag route with which it descended. It stood still and became so that no one could look directly at it. The masses were happy to still be alive, looking at each other saying "Miracle! Miracle!" Some laughed, others wept. The reporters wrote.

This view of the crowd, taken on October 13, 1917 during the Miracle of the Sun, shows some of the reaction. Witnesses agree that the sun began to spin and then started falling to the earth before returning to its natural position in the sky. The formerly rain-drench ground was immediately dried as were the clothes worn by those in attendance.

One of the principal anti-cleric publications of the day, a major Lisbon newspaper called *O Dia*, dispatched at least two of its reporters to the Cova da Iria to report on the culmination of what they believed was a great hoax being perpetrated on the faithful people of Portugal. Like their counterparts from *O*

---

[102] Ibid.

Seculo, they were there for the purpose of discrediting the children and exposing the incendiary lies that they had been spreading for the past six months. Now, in utter amazement, and with a feeling of undisclosed terror, they wrote on their notepads all that they had just witnessed. How could these events possibly be explained to the anti-clerics who governed the region? How would their own credibility be viewed if the truth of the miracle of Fatima were to be reported? Yet, could those events that their own eyes had witnessed be explained any other way?

Even some people who were not present at Cova da Iria that day reported witnessing the miracle. Credible witnesses such as the poet Affonso Lopes Vieira, who lived in S. Pedro de Moel, some 25 miles from Fatima, saw it from his home. A nine-year old boy, who would later grow to become Fr. Inacio Lourenco, saw it from Alburita approximately 12 miles away, as he walked from school with several of his classmates and their teacher, Dona Delfina Pereira Lopes. All of them observed the spectacle of the dancing sun that day. Fr. Lourenco would later write,

> *"It was like a globe of snow revolving on itself. Then suddenly it seemed to come down in a zigzag, threatening to fall on the earth. Terrified, I ran to shelter myself in the midst of the people. All were weeping, expecting from one moment to the next the end of the world. Near us was an unbeliever without religion, who had spent the morning mocking the blockheads who had made all that journey to Fatima to go and stare at a girl. I looked at him. He stood as if paralyzed, thunderstruck, his eyes fixed on the sun. Then I saw him tremble from head to foot, and raising his hands to heaven, he fell on his knees in the mire, shouting, Nossa Senhora! Nossa Senhora! Translated, Our Lady! Our Lady!*
> *Meanwhile the people continued to scream and cry out, begging God to pardon their sins. ...Afterwards we ran to the chapels of the town, which were filled in a few moments.*
> *During those long minutes of the solar phenomenon objects all about us reflected all the colors of the rainbow. As we*

looked at one another, one seemed blue, another yellow, another vermilion. ...All these strange phenomena increased the terror of the crowd. After about ten minutes the sun returned to its place in the same way it had descended, still pale and without splendor... "[103]

Lucia's sister Teresa was present on this day as well to witness the happenings. She again took note, as she had in August, that the sky was snowing flowers and emanating the same "rainbowlike light all over the ground and the people. The people looked up to see where the light was coming from," she said, "and they saw the sun spinning around." She also observed that "people could look at it as at the 'newly risen moon;' it was 'spinning down.'"[104] The spinning lasted for only a short time but what really captivated her attention was the falling flowers. They seemed to be "multicolored petals," she insisted, "but when they came close enough to see what they were, they disappeared."[105]

From her vantage point some distance back, Maria saw the same sundance that others were seeing, but a man standing next to her "said he saw a figure, a very beautiful form between two lights." After the Apparition, she also observed a man named Carlos Mendes, who later became the president of the municipality of Torres Novas, "put Lucia on his shoulder and carry her out to the crowd." He then had her stand on a rock and asked her to tell everyone what the "Blessed Virgin said." Lucia complied.[106]

[103] Ibid, page 149-150.
[104] McGlynn, Fr. Thomas, O.P., Vision of Fatima, Washington, DC., 1948. page 43-44.
[105] Ibid, page 45.
[106] Ibid, page 51.

PART IV
THE AFTERMATH

SATURDAY OCTOBER 13, 1917
3:00 PM – 11:00 PM

Many in the mass of 70,000 people began to leave, some to begin the long trek back home. Many others stayed and followed Lucia and her cousins hoping for maybe just a word with them and were still milling in the streets around their homes when Fr. Formigao arrived in Aljustrel at about 7:00 PM. He too wanted to speak to the children and hoped to do so before anyone else had a chance to speak with them and more importantly, before they could compare notes. Formigao was not present when the miracle occurred, but certainly had heard others speak of the amazing events of that afternoon. He used his authority to disperse the crowds and then gathered the children at the Marto home where he spoke to each separately. Except for the visions witnessed only by Lucia, their stories were virtually identical leaving some very minor discrepancies and one, relating to the size and rough age of the infant Jesus, that was of greater substance. Of course, Francisco could not hear the Lady so he could not testify as to what was said, rather only to what Lucia and Jacinta told him was said.

Fr. Formigao could see that the children were pale from exhaustion and agreed to return later to complete his examination. Eventually, everyone departed the area leaving behind trampled fields and no doubt talking about the miraculous events they had witnessed, comparing notes as to what one may have seen that another had not. For a short time, at least, the children could enjoy some time alone with family. Certainly, there was much to talk about!

SUNDAY OCTOBER 14, 2017

In addition to the *O Dia* reporters, several other newspaper reporters were present to witness the miracle, including a correspondent for the major

News Services in the United States. The following day, "from Lisbon, he cabled a long and impressive story about the Miracle of the Sun. Despite the enormity of the report, it was never published."[107] As Americans worried about the war and mourned the loss of some of the approximately 116 thousand Americans already counted among the war dead, baseball had become a most needed diversion. On October 13th, as Our Lady moved the sun in the Portugal sky, The Chicago White Sox, the hottest team in American baseball, having just completed an astounding regular season with a record of 100-54, were embroiled in game five of the 1917 World Series. The drama of the Series dominated the American newspapers and the White Sox dramatic 8-5 come-from-behind victory over the New York Giants in game five sent the series back to the Polo Grounds of New York for a game six.[108]

Save the events of World War I and the Baseball World Series, little else seemed to matter to the American people. In fact, twenty-five years would pass before whisperings of the Miracle at Fatima would begin to circulate around the United States.

Regardless of who else in the world took notice, the events of Saturday, October 13th were enough to finally convince Maria Rosa that something extraordinary had indeed happened to her daughter Lucia, her niece Jacinta and her nephew Francisco. When Teresa tried to tell her about the falling flowers that she witnessed in August, Maria Rosa dismissed her saying it was "ridiculous" and noting that her daughters were "all crazy." Yet after witnessing for herself the events that occurred just a few hours before, even a hardened critic such as she could no longer refute that something supernatural had occurred. Teresa said of her mother, "In October, she saw the wonders and then became convinced."[109]

---

[107] Walsh, William Thomas, Our Lady of Fatima, Image Book, Doubleday Publishing, 1954.
[108] https://en.wikipedia.org/wiki/1917_World_Series
[109] McGlynn, Fr. Thomas, O.P., Vision of Fatima, Washington, DC., 1948. page 45

MONDAY AND TUESDAY OCTOBER 15 - 16, 1917

Despite the lack of interest shown in the United States, there was no bigger news in Portugal, and for more than the next few days the people of Fatima were abuzz with what had occurred at the Cova on Saturday. Those who witnessed the great miracle were still in a state of utter amazement. Those that were now hearing about it second-hand had very mixed emotions. The faithful believed every utterance coming from the mouths of the eye witnesses while those naturally cynical toward such matters questioned each word stretching to find a logical reason for what they were being told.

WEDNESDAY, OCTOBER 17, 1917

Then on October 17th, *O Dia*, the major newspaper of the region, finally reported on the events that took place on Saturday, the thirteenth day of October, in the little hamlet of Fatima. The article read,

> *"A spectacle unique and incredible if one had not been a witness of it.... One can see the immense crowd turn toward the sun, which reveals itself free of the clouds in full noon. The great star of day makes one think of a silver plaque, and it is possible to look straight at it without the least discomfort. It does not burn, it does not blind, it might be like an eclipse. But now bursts forth a colossal clamor, and we hear the nearest spectators crying, 'Miracle, miracle! Marvel, marvel!'*
> *Before the astonished eyes of the people, whose attitude carries us back to biblical times and who, full of terror, heads uncovered, gaze into the blue of the sky, the sun has trembled, and the sun has made some brusque movements, unprecedented and outside of all cosmic laws-the sun has 'danced,' according to the typical expression of the peasants.....An old man whose stature and face, at once gentle and energetic, recall those of*

Paul Deroulede, turns toward the sun and recites the Credo with loud cries from beginning to end. I ask his name. It is Senhor Joao Maria Amado de Melo Ramalho da Cunha Vasconcelos. I see him afterwards addressing those about him who have kept their hats on, begging them vehemently to uncover before so extraordinary a demonstration of the existence of God. Similar scenes are repeated in all places.

The people ask one another if they have seen anything and what they have seen. The greatest number avow that they have seen the trembling and dancing of the sun. Others, however, declare that they have seen the smiling face of the Virgin herself; swear that the sun turned around on itself like a wheel of fireworks; that it fell, almost to the point of burning the earth with its rays. ...Another tells that he has seen it change color successively.... Almost three o'clock. The sky is limpid and the sun follows its course with its habitual brilliancy so that no one dares to look at it directly. And the shepherds?... Lucia, the one who speaks to the Virgin, announces with theatrical motions, on the neck of a man who carries her from group to group, that the war is going to end and that the soldiers are coming home. Such news, however, does not increase the joy of those who hear her. The celestial Sign, that is everything. Much curiosity, nevertheless, to see the two little girls with their garlands of roses; some try to kiss the hand of the 'little saints'" and one of the two, Jacinta, is much nearer to fainting than to dancing. But what all aspired for - the Sign in the Sky - has sufficed to satisfy them, to enroot them in their Breton-like faith....

Their dispersion follows rapidly and without incidents, without the shadow of disorder, without the need of any intervention of police patrols. The pilgrims who leave first, in haste to be on their way, are those who arrived first with their shoes on their heads or hung on their staves. They are going, their souls full of joy, to spread the good news in the villages that were not wholly depopulated to come here. And the priests? Some have shown themselves on the scene, standing rather with the curious spectators than in the company of pilgrims avid for celestial favors. Perhaps now and then one does not manage to conceal the satisfaction which appears so often on the faces of those who triumph. ...It remains for those competent to pronounce on the dance macabre of the sun, which today, at Fatima, has made hosannas burst from the breasts of the faithful and naturally has impressed - so witnesses worthy of belief assure me - even freethinkers and other persons not at all interested in religious matters who have come to this once famous countryside.[110]

The report quickly made its way throughout Portugal and beyond. For many of the more than 70,000 eye witnesses to the Miracle of the Sun, life regained some of its normalcy in the days that followed. Life for the children, on the other hand, had been irrevocably altered both mentally and spiritually.

FRIDAY, OCTOBER 19, 1917

The children were still quite fatigued when Fr. Formigao returned at the end of the week, and Lucia's memory of recent events during this round of questioning, was not as vivid as those of earlier events. Regardless, Formigao was convinced that the children had been honest with him and he became a believer in the reality of the Apparitions. He also began to defend the children against any adversary of the spiritual events. Despite his efforts, the persecution would come not only from the Freemasons and the Carbonari, but from other Catholics, including priests, as well. It was the former groups, however, who met secretly that week to formulate a strategy to not only defend against believers, but to launch a counter-attack as well.

---

[110] Walsh, William Thomas, Our Lady of Fatima, Image Book, Doubleday Publishing, 1954. page 147-148. Also, http://www.theholyrosary.org/fatimaapparitions.

TUESDAY, OCTOBER 23, 1917

On this night, several Freemason loyalists and other henchmen of the Administrator assembled in Ourem. Included in the group was a man known as Cemetery Frank. Armed with hatchets, axes and lanterns, the men loaded into several automobiles, and departed Ourem for the Cova da Aria where they intended to demolish any evidence of the Apparitions, including the holm-oak tree on which Our Lady appeared. They hoped that by destroying the relics, the rallying point of the faithful would be vanquished.

Upon arrival, the raiders chopped down the tree, and carried away anything that had been constructed or left at the site, including the table that Maria Carreira placed, and the lanterned arch that had been built there. After placing these items on display for a short time the marauders paraded them "through the streets, singing blasphemous litanies to the accompaniment of drums."[111]

WEDNESDAY, OCTOBER 24, 1917

Word of the "shrine's" destruction began to spread throughout the village creating anger from Moita to Aljustrel. Many, including Maria Carreira departed for the Cova, there to find the artifacts stolen as had been reported. However, to their joy, they learned that the raiders chopped down the wrong tree. The holm-oak tree on which Our Lady had appeared still stood proudly as an enduring symbol of the miracle at Fatima. The entire affair backfired on the Administrator as pilgrimage to the area increased. Maria Carreira returned frequently and one cold morning came upon a man who slept on the ground the entire night after walking thirty-eight miles to get there. When asked, the man told her, "I am glad I came. I feel very happy in this place."[112]

---

[111] Walsh, William Thomas, Our Lady of Fatima, Image Book, Doubleday Publishing, 1954. page 153.

[112] Ibid, page 155.

THE DAYS FOLLOWING OCTOBER 24, 1917

Over the ensuing days, Lucia's two parents would react quite differently to the miracle that they witnessed at the Cova. Antonio remained bitter that the large crowds had destroyed his land. Nothing could grow on the hard, trampled ground and planting, even on softened ground, would prove futile as the thousands of people who continued the pilgrimage to Fatima would crush them under foot anyway. For her part, Maria Rosa now believed that Lucia had told the truth and tried to comply with the requests of Our Lady as explained by her daughter. Recitations of the family Rosary became a nightly occurrence and Lucia was enrolled in a small day school that had recently been started by the monarchy near the church in Fatima. There she could learn to read and write as Our Lady asked. Much to Lucia's delight, Maria Rosa also convinced Olimpia to enroll Jacinta as well.

The children grew in devotion to Our Lady and Her message. They remained in prayer at virtually every opportunity. They often prayed at the Cova da Iria or the Cabeco and continued their efforts to avoid pilgrims though sometimes unsuccessfully. At times, their prayers resulted in cures or other miraculous happenings. Such was the case one day when the children were discovered by a group of curiosity seekers. Unable to hide, the children were surrounded and those present began to asked questions. One man picked Jacinta up and placed her on a wall so they could hear her better. Another tried to do the same to Francisco who was able to get away and climb on a different wall not too great a distance away. A woman from the parish of San Mamede, and her young son, approached Francisco and held out their arms to him pleading that he ask Our Lady to heal her sick husband and protect him from the war. Francisco began to say his Rosary and the crowd followed him in prayer. A short time later, they all moved to the Cova saying another Rosary along the way. The group eventually dispersed, but the woman returned a few days later to thank Our Lady. She was accompanied by her husband who had been restored to health.

Another day, Lucia's sister Teresa returned from Lomba, where she now lived with her husband, to ask Lucia to pray for the son of a woman who had been falsely accused of, and arrested for, a crime that he did not commit. He faced a long prison term and exile. Francisco, upon being told the story, was visibly upset and promised to pray at St. Anthony's Church while Jacinta and Lucia were in school. He was still kneeling in prayer when the girls returned from school. There, Francisco told Lucia that she could tell her sister that the boy would be released in a few days. On the thirteenth of the next month, the woman of Lomba made the trek to the Cova to give thanks to Our Lady for her son returned home just as Francisco said.

MAY 1918

Francisco desired nothing more on earth than to receive the "Hidden Jesus" in the Eucharist. Though a year older than Jacinta, they studied their catechism together beginning in the summer of 1917. Nine-year old Jacinta hoped to be granted permission to receive the sacrament prior to reaching the age of ten as local custom required. She knew exceptions could be made as Lucia was allowed to receive at the age of six.

In May of 1918, Manuel Marto presented his two children to Fr. Ferreira for questioning. Jacinta passed, but for the second time, Francisco did not. This time he cried as he knew his time on earth was short. Yet, he offered his disappointment in prayer saying, "It is for your love, O my Jesus!"[113]

Around this time, the local Bishops were completing their investigation of the apparitions of Fatima determining that "the apparitions were 'worthy of belief.'" Local residents immediately marked the site with a cross and, later in the year, a small chapel was built from rock and limestone and covered in tile. It was a very small structure measuring only 11 ft. by 9.2 ft. in length and 9.4 ft. in height, but it became the center for Marian devotion, receiving names such as *a fe Fatima, cidade da Paz* ("The faith of Fatima, City of Peace.") or *Terra de Milagres e Aparicoes* ("Land of Miracles and Apparitions.")[114]

---

[113] Ibid, page 159.
[114] https://en.wikipedia.org/wiki/F%C3%A1tima,_Portugal.

OCTOBER 1918

The influenza was a terrible scourge and had killed many throughout the world. In October of 1918 the Spanish flu pandemic found the little Village of Aljustrel.[115] All in the dos Santos family except Lucia were infected. Similarly, all in the Marto household save Manuel, were stricken with the virus. Manuel and Olimpia were heartbroken as Francisco became gravely ill. Though confined to his single iron bed with its patchwork quilt, ornate colored metal back topped off with two brass knobs, he complied with every request of his parents to eat, take his medicine, drink, etc. but promised them that it was to no avail as "Our Lady was coming to take him to heaven." He regretted only being unable to go to the Church of St. Anthony's to pray before the hidden Jesus.

A few days after Francisco, Jacinta became symptomatic complaining of a terrible headache and an insatiable thirst. Yet, she refused to drink because she wanted to suffer for sinners. Lucia spent every available moment with her when she wasn't in school or tending to her chores. One morning when Lucia stopped in to visit while on her way to school, Jacinta said, "Listen! Tell the Hidden Jesus that I like Him very much, that I really love Him very much indeed." On other days, she would ask Lucia to "tell Jesus that I send Him my love, and long to see Him."

As Our Lady promised the children, Francisco and Jacinta would go to heaven soon. Lucia dos Santos, on the other hand would remain on the earth a long time as God chose her to carry his message to the world.

---

[115] Ibid.

Yet, Jacinta was so unselfish that whenever Lucia visited her room first, Jacinta would tell her to "go and see Francisco" so she could make the sacrifice of "staying here alone."

One day when her mother brought her a cup of milk, Jacinta pushed it away with her hand saying she didn't want it. Jacinta's mother offered a little resistance then left the room saying, "I don't know how to make her take anything; she has no appetite." Lucia scolded Jacinta for disobeying her mother and not making the sacrifice for the Lord. At hearing this Jacinta cried. As Lucia wiped her tears, Jacinta said, "I forgot this time." She called her mother in the room as asked for forgiveness offering to take whatever her mother wanted her to take. When her mother returned with the milk, Jacinta drank it down with no sign of repugnance. Jacinta later told Lucia that it was very hard to drink that milk. As time went on, it became harder and harder for her to take milk and broth, but she didn't complain at all so she could suffer for love of the Lord, and the Immaculate Heart of Mary. Once, when Lucia asked Jacinta if she was getting better, she replied, "You know I'm not getting better. I've such pains in my chest! But I don't say anything. I'm suffering for the conversion of sinners." She even refrained from visiting Francisco's room as a sacrifice for the conversion of sinners.

During one visit, Lucia found Jacinta unusually elated. "Look, Lucia!" Jacinta noted, "Our Lady came to see us here, and she said that she is coming very soon to take Francisco to heaven. And she asked me if I still wanted to convert more sinners and I said yes. Our Lady wants me to go to two hospitals, but not to be cured. It is to suffer more for the love of God, for the conversion of sinners and in reparation for the offenses committed against the Immaculate Heart of Mary." Jacinta went on to say that it would be her mother, and not Lucia, who would take her to the hospital and then leave her there.[116]

After saying this Jacinta fell into thought for a while and added, "If only you could be with me! The hardest part is to go without you. Maybe, the hospital is a big dark house, where you can't see, and I'll be there suffering all alone! But never mind! I'll suffer for love of Our Lord, to make reparation to the Immaculate Heart of Mary, for the conversion of sinners and for the Holy Father."[117]

[116] Walsh, William Thomas, Our Lady of Fatima, Image Book, Doubleday Publishing, 1954. pages 161 - 162.
[117] Dos Santos, Sr. Lucia, Fatima in Lucia's Own Words. The Remembrances of Sister Lucia, 20th Edition, 2016. Pages 59-60.

DECEMBER 1918

The Marto family prayed fervently that their children might recover from their illness, but the children knew that was not to be. As December approached, however, Francisco's fever did begin to normalize and his pulse grew stronger and by Christmas he was able to get up for a short while each day until it looked like he may make a full recovery.

1919

JANUARY 1919

Following the Christmas and New Year's holidays, Francisco appeared at full strength. He began his daily routine of reciting the Angel's prayer at the Cabeco or the Rosary at the Cova da Iria. On one day, though suffering from a strong headache, he walked to Fatima where he knelt before the altar, consoling the hidden Jesus for quite some time. As much as he wanted only to pray, the pilgrims would not leave him alone. One day he returned home from prayer to find his house full of strangers asking that he bless their Rosaries, medals, crucifixes and other objects of prayer. They left only after he assured them that he was unable to bless anything as he wasn't a priest. He could hear some shout insults to him as they departed.

Before the calendar page turned to February Francisco was ill once again. Despite his family's attempts to make him think he would recover as he did before, he knew better. "Our Lady is coming very soon now," he told them. His godmother Teresa promised to tell Our Lady that she would offer Francisco's weight in wheat to the poor for the return of his health, but the boy responded, "It's not worth your trouble. Our Lady will not grant you this grace."[118] Just a few days later, Francisco's health declined radically and he found himself once again bed ridden. He was convinced that his body would

---

[118] Walsh, William Thomas, Our Lady of Fatima, Image Book, Doubleday Publishing, 1954. pages 162-163.

not leave the bed until he was taken to heaven and his health continued its downward slide.

JANUARY 1919 – MARCH 1919

Jacinta, meanwhile, never made such a temporary recovery, but despite her illness, she would sneak into Francisco's room when she was sure that no one else was in the house. There they would talk for as long as possible, that is, until her indiscretion was discovered and she was forbidden to repeat it. Lucia stopped in everyday on her way home from school to inquire of any sacrifices Jacinta made that day. It was, for the most part, the highlight of the little girl's day, able to tell Lucia how she refrained from going to Francisco's room even when everyone was out.

Francisco was in constant pain now, flushed with fever, his eyes large and bright, though rather than complain, he told Lucia that he accepted the pain as a means of consoling Our Lord. "When you go, don't forget to ask Our Lady to take me there soon also," Lucia said to her cousin. "I won't ask that," Francisco replied. "You know very well that She doesn't want you there yet."[119]

APRIL 1, 1919

When April began, Francisco was so weak that he couldn't even recite the Rosary. His mother suggested that he just say it in his heart noting that "Our Lady hears it just the same and is just as pleased."[120] This seemed to make him happy as he managed to purse his lips in an attempted smile. Francisco wanted to see Lucia and seemed desperate as he communicated this to his mother. Olimpia sent for Lucia at once and very soon thereafter, she was in Francisco's bedroom standing at his side. "Look, Lucia, I am very sick, and I am going to heaven very soon." He then conveyed a list of things he wanted Lucia to ask Jacinta

---

[119] Ibid, page 163.
[120] Ibid, page 164.

adding, "I want to go to confession," a wish Lucia conveyed to her aunt and uncle.

By nightfall, he was much worse and his parents promised to send word to the Rectory first thing in the morning asking the priest to come to hear their son's final confession.

APRIL 2, 1919

At dawn the following morning, Francisco asked his sister Teresa to get Lucia as he needed to speak with her at once. Awakened by Teresa at about 6:00 AM, Lucia dressed quickly and hurried to Francisco's bedside. Francisco asked his mother, brother John and two sisters to leave so he could share a secret with his cousin. They complied and Francisco told Lucia that he was going to confess his sins so that he could receive Communion and then die. "I want you to tell me if you have seen me commit any sin and ask Jacinta if she has seen me commit any."[121] After speaking with Jacinta, Lucia reported back to Francisco that Jacinta remembered that he had stolen a small coin from his father to purchase a hand-organ. Lucia recalled that he threw stones back at some children who first threw stones at him, and that he disobeyed his mother when she told him to stop staying in the house. Francisco renewed his sorrow for those sins, though acknowledging that he had previously confessed them and vowed to never repeat them even if he shall live. He then said an Act of Contrition.

APRIL 3, 1919

As the new day arrived, Francisco lay quietly awaiting the priest and opened his eyes only when he heard the ringing of the little bell signaling that the priest arrived with communion. Olimpia placed some lighted candles on a table near his bed and, though he was too weak to sit up, Francisco peered at

---

[121] Ibid, page 165.

the priest raising the Eucharist above him receiving Jesus in the Host for the first time as he lay dying in bed.

As Francisco's final hours drew near, Jacinta was allowed to visit his room. When he saw her he said, Today I am happier than you, for I have within my breast the hidden Jesus. I am going to heaven, but there I will pray a great deal to Our Lord and our Lady that they bring you there too, soon."[122] Jacinta remained with Francisco all day, sometimes helping him say the Rosary when he was too weak to do so and at other times, just looking at him while sitting at the edge of his bed. Lucia stopped by after school as well. They spoke for a while and Lucia, doubting that she might ever see him again, said, "Goodbye, Francisco. If you go to heaven tonight, don't forget me there, do you hear?" Taking her right hand in his, he said, "I won't forget you, no. Don't worry." Soon Lucia's aunt came to send her home. "Then goodbye, Francisco, till heaven. Goodbye till heaven," she repeated and left the room crying.

Before leaving his room, Jacinta whispered to her brother, "Give all my love to Our Lord and Our Lady and tell them that I'll suffer as much as they want, for the conversion of sinners and in reparation to the Immaculate Heart of Mary."

Francisco grew weaker by the minute so that by nightfall he could no longer take milk and despite his thirst could swallow only a few drops of water. Yet, when asked, he would say, "I'm all right, don't give me anything."[123]

10:00 AM, APRIL 4, 1919

His condition was relatively unchanged the following morning. Just prior to 10:00 AM, Francisco looked at his mother and asked forgiveness for any trouble he had caused her in his life and then he focused on the Eucharist he had received just a day prior. Francisco Marto died on April 4, 1919 in that hour passing almost without notice. There was still a faint smile on his lips when Jacinta and Lucia came to see his lifeless body lying on the bed.

---

[122] Ibid, page 166.
[123] Ibid, page 167.

APRIL 5, 1919

Several men from the Misericordia, walked slowly up the cobblestone road to Fatima. An acolyte carried a crucifix held high. He was followed by four boys dressed in white carrying a coffin containing the remains of Francisco as his grieving parents and a few others walked behind. Entering through the cemetery gate, the boys laid the small coffin down in a grave just inside the gate. Jacinta was still too sick to attend and Lucia went to the cemetery by herself later in the day placing a little cross on the grave.

Francisco Marto died on April 4, 1919, just short of two years after he first saw Our Lady of the Rosary. Just prior to his death, the eleven-year old boy asked his mother's forgiveness for any trouble he had caused her in his short life. His small casket was carried by four boys dressed in white.

APRIL 5, 1919 – JULY 1, 1919

Shortly after the death of Francisco, Jacinta was moved into the bed where he had died. It was a more convenient location and provided her an opportunity to see and hear people better as it was closer to the door. Lucia was a big comfort to her, especially in the early days following Francisco's death as Jacinta missed him terribly. She spent hours in thought and when asked said she was thinking about how much she missed her brother. As her eyes filled with tears she would say that she would "give anything to see him again." One day, Lucia said to Jacinta, "It won't be long now till you go to heaven, but what about me!" Jacinta comforted her saying, "You poor thing! Don't cry! I'll pray lots and lots for you when I'm there. As for you, that's the way Our Lady wants it. If she wanted that for me, I'd gladly stay and suffer more for sinners."

JULY – AUGUST 1919

Jacinta's health continued to deteriorate and was now punctuated by sharp pain in her chest cavity that worsened with each breath. The doctor said she had Pleurisy, a condition caused by inflammation of the linings around the lungs. Her thoughts drifted to the vision she had of Our Lady telling her that she would go to the hospital and be kept alone in a dark place until her death. She believed this would be her end, yet she also believed that, though incapacitated and perhaps removed for her family, she could still do much good.

She focused on helping others even while lying in excruciating pain. When Lucia's Aunt Victoria's brilliant, but erratic son couldn't be found for weeks, Jacinta prayed to Our Lady to deliver him safely home. After just a few days, he returned with a strange story indeed. It seems he had left home and spent all his money having to resort to theft for survival. He was eventually arrested and jailed in Torres Novas until one night when he found a means of escape. Fleeing to the mountains he hid there, but a terribly violent thunderstorm frightened him to prayer. Asking God's forgiveness, he fell to his knees praying in the rain for a safe return home. Shortly thereafter, he saw a small child emerge from the darkness. He recognized immediately that it was Jacinta as she took his hand and led him from the mountain on the road that leads from Alqueidao to Reguengo. At which point she made a sign that he should continue in that direction and then she vanished. The young man eventually came to a bridge that he recognized. It was near Boleiros, not far from where he lived in Fatima. After his safe return home, Lucia questioned Jacinta who said nothing of bilocation, admitting only that she "had prayed a great deal for the young man."[124]

The doctors advised Manuel and Olimpia Marto that their daughter would not recover at home and needed surgery and care that could be provided only in a hospital. She now had purulent pleurisy that resulted from the bronchial pneumonia. So, on a mid-July morning, Manuel lifted Jacinta on the back of a mule and took her to St. Augustine's Hospital in Vila Nove de Ourem. Upon admission, Jacinta realized that her room was bright and rather cheerful, not at all the dark place Our Lady indicated her mother would take her.

---

[124] Ibid, page 170.

Olimpia visited her and found her in good spirits with no complaints, although Jacinta mentioned how she longed to see Lucia. Lucia was having a bad summer too as her father Antonio became ill and died on July 31, 1919. Following her brother's death, Olimpia agreed to take Lucia with her to visit Jacinta, despite the hardship that it imposed. As soon as Jacinta saw Lucia she gave her a joyful hug. She asked her mother to leave Lucia in the hospital with her while her mother went shopping. She told Lucia, in response to her question, that she was indeed suffering a lot, but she "offers everything for sinners, and in reparation to the Immaculate Heart of Mary." Then, filled with enthusiasm, she spoke of Our Lord and Our Lady. 'Oh, how much I love to suffer for love of Them, just to give Them pleasure! They greatly love those who suffer for the conversion of sinners.'" As the allotted time for the visit ended, Jacinta asked her mother to bring Lucia again next visit, which she gladly did. That visit found Jacinta just about the same, happy to suffer for the love of our Good God and the Immaculate Heart of Mary, for sinners and for the Holy Father. "That was her ideal and she could speak of nothing else."[125]

AUGUST 31, 1919

Jacinta's health did not much improve following her surgery, in fact, it worsened and she still suffered a great deal of pain, but the Martos were out of money. Manuel did his best, but could no longer afford the $1.35 it cost him for each day Jacinta remained in the hospital. On the last day of August, Manuel checked her out of St. Augustine's in Vila Nova de Ourem returning Jacinta home to their care for a while. She had a large surgical wound in her chest which had to be treated every day, and she was almost unrecognizable; very thin, looking pale and emaciated, but she bore the transfer without complaint.

[125] Dos Santos, Sr. Lucia, Fatima in Lucia's Own Words. The Remembrances of Sister Lucia, 20th Edition, 2016. Pages 60-61.

OCTOBER 13, 1919

During her days at home Jacinta's health failed even more rapidly. By October, she had developed tuberculosis and Dr. Formigao came to see her. He had made the pilgrimage, along with 600 faithful people, to the Cova da Iria on the second anniversary of the great miracle. He found Jacinta as "a living skeleton, her arms nothing but bones, her face all eyes, her cheeks wasted by fever." Yet he could do nothing but suggest placement in a really good sanitarium.

Surprisingly though, Jacinta's health improved during the warm days of autumn allowing her to leave her bed, go outside and even attend Mass at Fatima on Sunday. Much to her delight, she was even able to venture to Cova da Iria a time or two. Her parents were understandably upset when they discovered that she had done this and put a stop to it immediately much to the chagrin of little Jacinta. As the first blast of cold air arrived, however, her fever returned leaving Jacinta bedridden once again. She accepted this cheerfully as she was still able to prostrate herself and recite the Rosary each day, but eventually, even this became difficult. She confided in Lucia, "When I am alone I get out of bed to say the prayers of the Angel, but now I can't put my head on the floor anymore, because I fall, so I pray only on my knees."[126] With each passing day Jacinta grew closer to Jesus and Mary in prayer and sacrifice and on three different occasions, Our Lady appeared to Jacinta in her bedroom and spoke to her with words of encouragement.

DECEMBER 1919

The final of these appearances occurred in December 1919 and Our Lady spoke to Jacinta of "new crosses and sacrifices awaiting her."[127] "Our Lady came to see me last night," Jacinta told Lucia, "and told me that I am going to Lisbon to another hospital; that I will not see you again, nor my parents either, and after

---

[126] Walsh, William Thomas, Our Lady of Fatima, Image Book, Doubleday Publishing, 1954. pages 174.

[127] Dos Santos, Sr. Lucia, Fatima in Lucia's Own Words. The Remembrances of Sister Lucia, 20th Edition, 2016. Pages 62.

suffering a great deal, I shall die alone. But she said I must not be afraid, since she herself is coming to take me to heaven." The two hugged and Jacinta wept, "I will never see you again! You won't be coming to visit me there. Oh please, pray hard for me, because I am going to die alone!"

Dying alone seemed to be her biggest fear. One day Lucia brought Jacinta a stamp on which was a picture of the Mother of Sorrows. Jacinta gazed upon it with an anguished look on her face and then began to cry. "Oh, my little Mother of Heaven," she sobbed with a tear-soaked face, "do I really have to die alone?" But when reminded that Our Lady would take her personally to Heaven, she would find total comfort.

Jacinta also lamented having to die without receiving the hidden Jesus wishing that "Our Lady would bring Him to me, when she comes to fetch me!" One-day Lucia asked Jacinta what she would do in Heaven. "I'm going to love Jesus very much, and the Immaculate Heart of Mary, too. I'm going to pray a lot for you, for sinners, for the Holy Father, for my parents and my brothers and sisters, and for all the people who have asked me to pray for them..." When she noticed her mother looking sad at seeing her child so sick, Jacinta would comfort her saying, "Don't worry, mother. I'm going to Heaven, and there I'll be praying so much for you," or "Don't cry. I'm alright." She would always refuse offerings but would later tell Lucia how she refused only as a sacrifice for sinners. Yet Jacinta insisted that Lucia never tell her mother how much she was suffering so as not to upset her.[128]

EARLY JANUARY 1920

Right up until the day of her departure for the hospital in Lisbon, the smallest visionary suffered great anguish at the thought of never seeing Lucia or her family again, and of dying without them... alone. Lucia advised her not to think about it. "Let me think about it," Jacinta responded, "for the more I think the more I suffer, and I want to suffer for love of Our Lord and for sinners. Anyway, I don't mind! Our Lady will come to me there and take me to heaven." At other times, she would kiss and embrace the crucifix saying as she did, "O

---

[128] Ibid, pages 62-62.

my Jesus! I love you, and I want to suffer very much for love of You." She very often said, "O Jesus! Now You can convert many sinners, because this is a really big sacrifice!"

The thought of never seeing Jacinta again caused Lucia to suffer greatly as well though no one other than Lucia really took the talk of hospitals in Lisbon very seriously. Lisbon was, after all, a ninety-mile trip and the Martos knew that they could not afford another hospital stay for Jacinta even if it were required. That all changed in January 1920 when an automobile pulled up to the Marto home. Manuel and Olimpia watched with curiosity as Dr. Formigao exited the vehicle with two strangers who turned out to be noted ophthalmologist Dr. Enrico Lisboa and his wife. Dr. Formigao had spoken much of little Jacinta to Dr. Enrico who had taken a special interest in her case. A quick examination was all the doctor needed to understand that the girl would die without the care provided in a hospital. He used his connections and along with a few of his friends acting as financial benefactors, was able to arrange for the hospital stay.

JANUARY 20, 1920

While this all came as somewhat of a shock to the family, Jacinta was expecting it and actually felt better now that it was happening. While awaiting the necessary arrangements to be made by the doctor and his friends, Jacinta convinced her mother, who along with a neighbor, took the little girl to the Cova da Iria for one last visit. There, they knelt to say the Rosary. Afterward, Jacinta picked some wild flowers which she carefully placed in the little chapel that had been built where the holm-oak stood. With this offering, she knelt by the small tree to say a prayer, then after being helped up by her mother, mounted the mule for the journey home.

JANUARY 21, 1920

The very next morning, Jacinta said goodbye to her father and then, turning to Lucia, hugged her very tightly. Lucia's heart broke and she held her little cousin in her arms for a long time. Both cried as Jacinta said, "We shall never meet again. Pray for me a lot till I go to heaven, and afterwards I'll pray a lot for you. Never tell anybody the secret even if they kill you. Love Jesus and the Immaculate Heart of Mary a great deal and make many sacrifices for sinners. Goodbye, Lucia."

Jacinta was taken to the train station by her mother and older brother Antonio who accompanied her on the trip, a train ride that took four to five-hours and was very taxing for Jacinta. In Lisbon, they were met by three well-dressed ladies that turned out to be friends of the Baron. After many hours, they finally secured lodging where Olimpia, Jacinta and Antonio remained for a week after which time a more permanent place was found at the Catholic orphanage near the Church of Our Lady of Miracles, run by a Franciscan nun by the name of Dona Maria da Purificacao Godinho.[129] Madre Godinho had a special devotion to Our Lady and had longed to meet the children to whom She appeared. Upon learning that one of the children was now in her care, she took the child to her heart like a mother, placing Jacinta each day by the sunny window overlooking the Garden of the Estrela.

Jacinta enjoyed living in the convent especially knowing that the hidden Jesus had a home there as well. She attended Mass and received the hidden Jesus every day and on quick order, Mother Godinho believed that a saint was living under her roof. She noticed how Jacinta avoided the other girls except to give them motherly advice on obedience and truthfulness. She spoke with authority and the nun would sometime draw her into conversation and carefully write down some of the more striking things the child would say.

One-day Jacinta noted to Mother Godinho, "Our Lady wants my sisters Teresa (15 years of age) and Florinda (16 years of age) to be nuns. My mother doesn't want them to be, but for this Our Lady will take them to heaven before long."[130]

---

[129] Dos Santos, Sr. Lucia, Fatima in Lucia's Own Words. The Remembrances of Sister Lucia, 20th Edition, 2016. Pages 63.

[130] Walsh, William Thomas, Our Lady of Fatima, Image Book, Doubleday Publishing, 1954. pages 180.

FEBRUARY 2 – FEBRUARY 9, 1920

Despite Jacinta's enjoyment of life in the convent, her stay there was short. On February 2nd, the Feast of the Purification of Our Lady, she was transferred to the Hospital of Dona Stefania as prophesied by the Blessed Mother. Jacinta was assigned Bed 38, on the first floor of this rather dark, depressing place. Noted pediatrician and chief surgeon, Dr. Castro Freire, conducted a thorough examination confirming the diagnosis of purulent pleurisy that required another operation just as soon as little Jacinta was strong enough to handle it. "It won't do any good," Jacinta warned, "Our Lady came to tell me that I am going to die soon."[131]

Jacinta was delighted one day as she looked up to see her father standing over her. He had made the long journey but had only a few hours to remain because some of his other children were sick and he was needed back home. She told him to let Lucia know that Our Lady had visited her in the hospital and told her the day and hour of her death.[132] Jacinta also knew a great deal of other information told her by Our Lady and she shared those prophecies with others from time to time.

Mother Godinho, for example, visited Jacinta daily. On one particular day Godinho told her about a dynamic sermon delivered by a certain priest, one that was praised by fashionable ladies because of his theatrical voice and kind manner. Jacinta said, "When you least expect it, you will see that that priest is wicked." Just a few months later, the orator left the priesthood under rather scandalous circumstances.

On another occasion, Jacinta told a doctor who had asked for her prayers when she reached heaven that he and his daughter would die shortly after she passed; and they did. "To mother Godinho, who wanted to visit Cova da Iria; she said, "You will go -- but after my death; and so will I."

In fact, the extraordinary girl revealed during this time a great many little-known, but remarkable statements made by Our Lady, including:

---

[131] https://www.ewtn.com/fatima/jacinta-marto.asp.
[132] Dos Santos, Sr. Lucia, Fatima in Lucia's Own Words. The Remembrances of Sister Lucia, 20th Edition, 2016. page 63.

"More souls go to hell because of sins of the flesh than for any other reason; Certain fashions will be introduced that will offend Our Lord very much; Many marriages are not good - they do not please Our Lord and are not of God; Priests must be pure, very pure - they should not busy them-selves with anything except what concerns the Church and souls; The disobedience of priests to their superiors and to the Holy Father is very displeasing to Our Lord; The Blessed Mother can no longer restrain the hand of her Divine Son from striking the world with just punishment for its many crimes; Tell everybody that God gives graces through the Immaculate Heart of Mary; Tell them to ask graces from her, and that the Heart of Jesus wishes to be venerated together with the Immaculate Heart of Mary."[133]

FEBRUARY 10, 1920

Jacinta was taken into surgery on February 10th, but her condition had so weakened her that the doctors could not use the chloroform or ether before performing the surgery and opted instead to use a local anesthesia. Dr. Castro Freire opened her left side and removed two ribs leaving a gap wide enough for him to insert his hands. The pain was excruciating and the child yelled, "Ai, Nossa Senhora!"[134] Then she murmured, "Patience! We ought to suffer every-thing to go to heaven... It is for your love, my Jesus!... Now you can convert many sinners, for I suffer much."[135]

---

[133] http://www.theholyrosary.org/fatimaapparitions.

[134] The Portuguese word "Ai" is an expression or yell/call of distress. Jacinta, then, was calling out in distress for Our Lady.
[135] Walsh, William Thomas, Our Lady of Fatima, Image Book, Doubleday Publishing, 1954. pages 181.

When the surgery was complete, the doctors felt success and Jacinta was returned to the same ward but was placed in Bed 60. Jacinta knew, however, that she would not recover and that her end was near though she suffered great pain for many additional days.

FEBRUARY 16, 1920

On this day Mother Godinho visited her special friend yet again and this time was told that Our Lady had appeared to her to say, "She was coming for me very soon and would take away my pains."[136]

FRIDAY, FEBRUARY 20, 1920
6:00 – 8:00 PM

By this time Jacinta knew her time was near as Our Lady had informed her when her last day and hour would be. She called for her nurse, Aurora Gomez, at 6:00 PM to request the last sacraments. Two hours later, Father Pereira dos Reis of the Church of the Holy Angels arrived to give the holy child the last rites of the Catholic Church. He promised to return the following morning to bring her Communion as well.

10:30 PM

Jacinta knew well, however, that she wouldn't be there in the morning. Nurse Gomez stepped out of her room for just a few moments. It was then that the Mother of God reached down to Bed 60 and took little Jacinta into her arms for her final journey, her suffering complete, her eternal happiness before her. Jacinta must have finally felt comfort in the arms that once held the baby Jesus

---

[136] Ibid.

for as the nurse returned, she saw Jacinta "breath her last sigh, a rosy flush on her cheeks, a half smile on her lips."[137]

FEBRUARY 22, 1920

The news of Jacinta's death spread quickly and some of the faithful raised funds to support the funeral expenses. Burial would be at a cemetery in Lisbon. She was dressed in a white communion dress with a blue cape displaying the colors of Our Lady. Her body was placed in a white coffin and taken to the Church of the Holy Angels. There it was carefully placed in the sacristy across two small benches. So many people came to the church that it became necessary for Pastor Pereira dos Reis to drive them out of the sacristy and request that the body be taken to Casa do Despacho of the brotherhood of the Most Blessed Sacrament, where he locked the door and turned the key over to undertaker Antonio Rebelo de Almeida. When Baron de Alvaiazere offered a grave in his plot in a cemetery in Ourem, the burial plans changed and the original burial site in Lisbon was abandoned.

FEBRUARY 23-24, 1920

Prior to applying the permanent seal to the casket, the undertaker allowed a few people to view the remains. All agreed that the body emanated an odor of flowers, and some insisted that the body still had flushed cheeks giving the impression of life. The next day the casket was sealed, transported from Rossio to Chao de Macas by train and then driven by automobile to Ourem. Only a few people from Aljustrel could make the journey to Ourem for the funeral, but among them was a very distraught Manuel Marto who repeated

---

[137] Dos Santos, Sr. Lucia, Fatima in Lucia's Own Words. The Remembrances of Sister Lucia, 20th Edition, 2016. page 63. Also, Walsh, William Thomas, Our Lady of Fatima, Image Book, Doubleday Publishing, 1954. pages 182.

through his tears over and over: "And you died there alone!" Olimpia and Lucia, though unable to attend the funeral services, eventually journeyed together to Ourem to visit the tiny grave of their beloved daughter and cousin.

The anti-clerics, for their part, were concerned only about any resulting devotion to this religious nonsense and immediately began to circulate rumors that the Catholic Church had both Francisco and Jacinta murdered to avoid contradictions in the stories of the three children of Fatima, of whom, only Lucia, and her version of events, remained. Despite their efforts, the many devout followers of Our Lady of Fatima resolved to vindicate the honor of the children.

AUGUST 5, 1920

The nation of Portugal was in a miserable state in 1920, politically, economically and morally, but the worse had not yet come. Between 1910 and 1926 there would be sixteen political revolutions and the government would change forty-three times. Those governments perpetuated revolts against Christianity. Pope Benedict XV noted in 1920 that "Morals are much more depraved and corrupt than formerly. The fond hope and wish of every renegade is the speedy rise of some universal state which is based on the complete equality of men and women and common ownership of property as a fundamental principle, in which neither any distinctions of nationality nor authority of parents over children, nor of public authority over citizens, nor of God over man living in society, is acknowledged. If these principles are put into practice, dreadful horrors must necessarily follow.[138].

Through the chaos, a new bishop was consecrated as head of the new diocese of Leiria. This area included all the Serra in which lay the Cova da Iria and Aljustrel. Pope Benedict had now made this an independent jurisdiction with the intelligent and charming Dom Jose Alves Correira as its vicar. At the time of his appointment, Correira served as a professor at the Seminary of Porto, but in his earlier days, suffered greatly at the hands of the Republic that

---

[138] Motu Propio, Bonum Sane, July 25, 1920, taken from Walsh, William Thomas, Our Lady of Fatima, Image Book, Doubleday Publishing, 1954. Pages 188

tortured him by forcing him to stand, day and night, in ice water. The experience left Correira permanently disabled.

AUGUST 6, 1920 – JUNE 12, 1921

Though the new bishop was no stranger to suffering, this assignment presented a new challenge as the years of religious persecution at the hands of the Freemason government left many of the clerics scattered, exiled and without a source of income. The new diocese was dead broke and even large numbers of parishioners "had given up Mass and the sacraments."[139] With the hope of revitalization of the new diocese, one of Bishop Correira's first acts was the consecration of his diocese to the Blessed Mother, and he did this symbolically on the feast of the Assumption in 1920. Shortly thereafter, Maria Carreira presented him with the funds collected at the site of the Fatima Apparitions, an amount that had now grown to some 357,000 reis, requesting that he use the money as he wished. This would prove no easy task as there were many forces at work, some faithful believers in the Apparitions of Fatima and others, including some priests, who argued that it was a delusion. Bishop Correira also had to consider the fodder that the use of such funds would provide to the enemies of the Church.

The new Bishop also faced the dilemma of Lucia. He believed that the anti-clerics posed a threat to her life because she was the sole survivor of the three visionaries, but also knew that many believers wanted to see her canonized into sainthood. As he wrestled with these issues, he sent word to Maria Rosa to bring Lucia to see him on June 13, 1921.

---

[139] Walsh, William Thomas, Our Lady of Fatima, Image Book, Doubleday Publishing, 1954. pages 189.

JUNE 13, 1921

Maria Rosa complied with the Bishop's request arriving at his home at the appointed hour. After making idle chat for a short while, Bishop Correira asked Lucia if she might like to leave Aljustrel for an opportunity to attend a good school where she could fulfill Our Lady's wishes by learning to read and write. Lucia was intrigued with the idea also realizing that a fresh start in a new place would help her with her grief. It might also put an end to the many visitors with their endless questions. Maria Rosa also liked the idea as such a move would reduce her stress as well. Their favorable reaction pleased the Bishop who suggested that Lucia could enter a school near Porto run by the Sisters of Saint Dorothy. He also suggested that she leave right away and tell no one where she was going. Additionally, she was to tell no one at the new school who she was. Nor was she to speak of the Apparitions! To these requirements Lucia readily agreed.

JUNE 18, 1921

Lucia's last day in Aljustrel was taken up with visits to family and friends. She offered her goodbyes, yet complied with the Bishop's request to tell no one where she was going. Afterward, Lucia visited the Cabeco where the Angel had first appeared. She prostrated herself at the cave beside the rock where He had knelt and repeated the prayer He had given her. Rising to her feet, Lucia climbed over the rocks and down the slope to Valinhos to the site of the August 19, 1917 Apparition of Our Lady. Fieldstones now encircled the holm-oak tree on which She appeared. Lucia knelt beside the "shrine" and cried in grief for her two cousins and in love of Our Lady. She believed that she may never see this place again and found leaving very difficult. Finally, the sole-surviving visionary made her way to the Cova da Iria, walking to the holm-oak tree that once held the weight of Our Lady. She knelt, alone, recalling the words of encouragement spoken to her by the Mother of God. *"I am the Lady of the*

Rosary.... Do you suffer a great deal? Don't be discouraged. I will never for-sake you. "[140]

Lucia left for home, interrupting her journey for just three additional stops. One at St. Anthony's Church so she might say one final prayer there. A second at the grave of her cousin Francisco so she could say a last goodbye to him, and fi-nally, to the home of her Aunt Olimpia and Uncle Manuel. In just two years they lost not only Francisco and Jacinta, but also their daughters Florinda and Teresa who died in 1920 and 1921 respectively, just as Jacinta had prophesied to Mother Godinho back in January of 1919. She bid them farewell, said a prayer in the room where Francisco had died, and left their home for hers with tear-filled eyes. She spent a few minutes at the well, ate supper, and went to bed.

JUNE 19, 1921
2:00 AM

Lucia heard her mother call. It was still very early -- 2:00 in the morn-ing, but Manuel Carreira waited outside with the cart to take them to Porto. They stopped briefly at the Chapel where they said the Rosary then departed for the nine-hour journey.

11:00 AM

Arriving in Leiria, the travelers were met by a lady that the Bishop had sent. She took them the rest of the way to the train station where she and Lucia boarded the train bound first for Alfarelos and then for Porto. "Goodbye," Ma-ria Rosa shouted to her fourteen-year old daughter. She wiped away her tears as the train slowly pulled away from the station.

---

[140] Ibid, page 192.

JUNE 20, 1919 – OCTOBER 24, 1925

Lucia and her guide arrived at the Asilo of the Sisters of Saint Dorothy at Vilar early on the morning of June 20th. The daily Mass was already in progress and Lucia was in time to receive Holy Communion. Following Mass, Lucia was led to the sacristy where she was introduced to both the Chaplain and the Mother Superior, the latter of whom was doing a favor, against her better judgment, for her friend Bishop Correira.

"When they ask your name," Mother Superior said, "you will reply, 'Call me Maria of the Sorrows.' When they ask you where you are from you will say, 'I am from near Lisboa.' As for what happened at Fatima, never again mention it to anyone, either by question or by answer. Not to anyone. Do you understand?" Lucia was compliant. "You will not go to walk with the other girls, but you will not say why you do not go. Do you understand, my dear?" Mother Superior continued. "Yes, Reverend Mother," Lucia responded. "That is all," Mother Superior said with a dismissive wave of her hand.

Lucia was led to her room where she would spend the better part of the next four years in patient compliance. Each day started with the Holy Mass, then a series of classes, then recreation followed by some manual work, prayers, and finally more schoolwork. Over the four years Lucia learned to embroider, sew, type, and cook. She spent many hours scrubbing floors, polishing brass and silver and waiting on tables. She kept her identity secret as instructed and never spoke of Fatima, not even to her mother who visited her a couple of times.

Over the years Lucia had come to love the convent and those who devoted their lives to the labor of helping to educate her. She found peace there and appreciated that the Bishop had sent her. She earned the respect and love of the others as they saw in her the unselfishness and extraordinary devotion to God that so characterized her.

Now, however, at eighteen years of age, it was time for Lucia to leave the convent school and enter the real world. She initially opted for the very difficult life of the Discalced Carmelites, but followed Mother Superior's advice against it. Eventually, she decided to enter the order of the Sisters of Saint Dorothy so that she would have more free time to go to the chapel and pray. And so, on October 24, 1925, Lucia joined the order as a postulant in Tuy, just across the border into Spain.

1925
DECEMBER 10, 1925

During her Appearance to the children on July 13, 1917, Our Lady promised Lucia that She would return

"to ask for the consecration of Russia to my Immaculate Heart, and the Communion of Reparation on the First Saturdays." She also promised, *"If my requests are heeded, Russia will be converted and there will be peace. If not, she will spread her errors throughout the world, causing wars and persecution of the Church. The good will be martyred, the Holy Father will have much to suffer, various nations will be annihilated. In the end, my Immaculate Heart will triumph. The Holy Father will consecrate Russia to me, and she will be converted, and a period of peace will be granted to the world."*

No doubt Lucia wondered throughout the past eight years what Our Lady meant by that message. On this day she would find out, as December 10, 1925 held the partial fulfillment of that promise. While sitting in her cell at the convent, Sister Lucia saw a familiar vision of "the most holy Virgin, and by her side, elevated on a luminous cloud, was a Child." The Mother of God rested her hand on Lucia's shoulder, simultaneously revealing a heart encircled by thorns that She held in her other hand. The Child Jesus spoke first saying

"Have compassion on the Heart of which ungrateful men pierce at every moment, and there is no one to make an act of reparation to remove them." As the Child finished, His most holy Mother said, *"Look, my daughter, at my Heart surrounded by thorns with which ungrateful men pierce me every moment by their blasphemies and ingratitude. You, at least, try to console me and say that I promise to assist, at the hour of death, with the graces necessary for salvation of all those who,*

on the first Saturday of five consecutive months, shall go to confession, receive Holy Communion, recite five decades of the Rosary, and keep me company for fifteen minutes while meditating on the fifteen mysteries of the Rosary with the intention of making reparation to me. "[141]

From this point on, Our Lady would return to Lucia at regular intervals to instruct her further and to offer her comfort. Perhaps to create an atmosphere appropriate for such visitations Lucia sought and obtained permission from her superiors and confessor to pray alone in the chapel every Thursday and Friday night from eleven o'clock until midnight. At least one of the future Apparitions would take place in this setting.

1927
DECEMBER 17, 1927

Our Lady appeared to Lucia once again on December 17, 1927 this time granting permission for Lucia to reveal the first two parts of the message of Fatima. These include the visions of the Angel; the promise to take the children to Heaven; the vision of hell; the predictions of another war, martyrdom for Christians, the destruction of nations, the persecution of the Church and of the Holy Father, and the spread of Communism. Until now, none of the children had revealed any part of the secrets.

---

[141] http://www.theholyrosary.org/fatimaapparitions. Also, The Great Promise of the Heart of Mary, Imprimatur: Fatima, January 13, 2007.

1929
JUNE 13, 1929
BETWEEN 11:00 PM AND MIDNIGHT

Sometime before the clock struck Midnight on June 13, 1929, Our Lady returned to Lucia to fulfill a promise made to her over a decade ago during the July 13, 1917 Apparition; the promise to *"...come to ask for the consecration of Russia."* While Lucia prayed alone in the Chapel of Dorotheas in the town of Tuy, she knelt in the middle of the darkened chapel near the altar rails. Prostrating herself, she prayed in the words of the Angel. After a time, she was overcome with fatigue and stood to complete her prayers with outstretched arms as if on a cross. Despite the room being lit with only the sanctuary light, the whole chapel was suddenly "illumined by a supernatural light, and above the altar appeared a cross of light, reaching to the ceiling. In a brighter light on the upper part of the cross, could be seen the face of a man and his body as far as the waist, upon his breast was a dove of light, nailed to the cross was the body of another man."

Lucia discerned a little above the Man's waist, a chalice and a large host suspended in the air, "on to which drops of blood were falling from the face of Jesus Crucified and from the wound in His side. These drops ran down onto the host and fell into the chalice. Beneath the right arm of the cross was Our Lady and in Her hand, was her Immaculate Heart. (It was Our Lady of Fatima, with her Immaculate Heart in her left hand, without sword or roses, but with a crown of thorns and flames. Under the left arm of the cross, large letters, -as if of crystal clear water which ran down upon the altar, formed these words: 'Grace and Mercy'."

Lucia understood this to be the Mystery of the Most Holy Trinity revealed, and she received insights about this mystery which she was not permitted to reveal. Our Lady then said to Lucia,

"The moment has come in which God asks the Holy Father, in union with all the Bishops of the world, to make the consecration of Russia to my Immaculate Heart, promising to

save it by this means. There are so many souls whom the justice of God condemns for sins committed against me, that I have come to ask reparation. Sacrifice yourself for this intention and pray.' "[142]

This vision and the words of Our lady were discussed with, and formally submitted to, Lucia's superiors. They in turn, made sure the message reached the appropriate authorities who could determine the appropriateness of alerting the Pope.

1935
SEPTEMBER 12 – DECEMBER 15

It seemed that the years had begun to tie up any loose ends in the wake of the Apparitions to the children, regardless of where those Apparitions took place. Jacinta had been promised that she would one day, after her death, return to Fatima and it appeared that the year 1935 would bring the fulfillment of that promise. The small casket carrying Jacinta's remains was exhumed from its original burial spot in a cemetery at Vila Nova de Ourem some fifteen and a half years later. On September 12, 1935, the casket was taken to the cemetery in Fatima where Jacinta could be reunited with her brother Francisco. Prior to her reburial, the casket was opened to the audible sound of many gasps from those present. To the amazement of many, the body, it seems, was found to be completely intact, a state referred to as uncorrupted. Various photographs were taken of the body, one of which was sent by Bishop Jose Alves Correira da Silva to Lucia.[143]

---

[142] Schulte, Paul C. Archbishop of Indianapolis, Our Lady of Fatima's "Peace Plan From Heaven" January 15, 1950, Page 13-14. Also http://www.theholy-rosary.org/fatimaapparitions.
[143] Dos Santos, Sr. Lucia, Fatima in Lucia's Own Words. The Remembrances of Sister Lucia, 20th Edition, 2016. page 33. Also, McGlynn, Fr. Thomas, O.P., Vision of Fatima, Washington, DC., 1948. page 217.

The photo was received by a thankful Lucia on November 17th and she immediately wrote a thank you note to the Bishop in which she recalled some very vivid memories of Jacinta. Upon reading her note, it occurred to Bishop Correira that Lucia had a great deal of information about her cousin that no one else knew and he worried that all that information might be forever lost if anything were to happen to her. Hoping to preserve Jacinta's memory, he sent word to Lucia requesting that she reduce to writing everything she could still remember about her.[144]

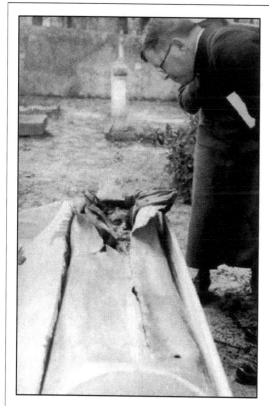

After suffering greatly, Jacinta Marto was taken to heaven by Our Lady on Friday February 20, 1920. Her body was buried in a cemetery in Ourem but was exhumed on September 12, 1935 for reburial in the same cemetery in Fatima in which Francisco's body lay. Though having been in the ground for over 15 years, her body was found to be incorrupt and giving off a fragrance of flowers.

---

[144] Dos Santos, Sr. Lucia, Fatima in Lucia's Own Words. The Remembrances of Sister Lucia, 20th Edition, 2016. page 33.

Lucia received the message on December 15th and immediately began to pen a memoir on Jacinta as Bishop Correira had requested. In this memoir, Lucia wrote of Jacinta's life but was careful to not reveal any of the secrets shared by Our Lady with the children.[145] The Bishop read the memoir with great interest and shared it with Fr. Fonseca. After reading Lucia's account of Jacinta, the vivid memories, and the extraordinarily detailed information that was contained within, Fr. Fonseca, wrote to the Bishop on November 7th noting that Lucia's "first memoir makes one think that there are further interesting details in the history of the Apparitions...which are not yet known. Consequently, he asked the Bishop to ask Lucia to write down everything she remembers about the Apparitions.

Bishop Jose concurred with Fr. Fonseca's request and "gave Lucia the necessary order." Lucia immediately replied to the Bishop that she had "begun today, for this is the Will of God." Just three weeks later, on November 21st, Lucia completed the 38-page manuscript, filled front and back with close handwriting, almost without corrections, as requested by the Bishop. This manuscript revealed much of the detail that had been missing about the angelic apparitions, her extraordinary blessings on the occasion of her First Communion, the Immaculate Heart of Mary in the Apparition of June 1917, and much more.

In addressing her reluctance to share the information asked to be kept secret by Our Lady, she writes a note to God saying, "No longer will I savor the joy of sharing with You alone the secrets of Your love, but henceforth, others too, will sing the greatness of Your mercy... Behold the handmaid of the Lord! May He continue to make use of her, as He thinks best."

1938
JANUARY 25 AND 26

On the night of January 25, 1938, Sister Lucia stood by the window in her room at the convent. She noticed a red glow, an ominous glow, that seemed to light the entire sky. Lucia was not the only one to see this light, however, as it was visible throughout Europe and Africa and in parts of America and Asia.

---

[145] Ibid.

The lights persisted and continued to light the sky the following night as well. It was explained scientifically as the lights of the aurora borealis despite the northern lights being a most unusual occurrence in Portugal.

Lucia dos Santos was only ten-years old when Our Lady told her that she would remain on earth well after the deaths of her cousins so that she could establish devotion in the world to Mary's Immaculate Heart. Sister Lucia's mission ended on February 13, 2005, less than two months shy of her 98th birthday.

Lucia knew better however, sensing immediately that she had just witnessed the fulfillment of Our Lady's prophecy of July 13, 1917 in which she promised *"When you see the night illumined by an unknown light, know that this is the great sign given you by God that he is about to punish the world for its crimes, by means of war, famine, and persecutions of the Church and of the Holy Father."* She made arrangement to see that the Pope was informed of her belief.

Pius XII was the Pontiff as World War II was officially begun on September 1, 1939 following the declarations of war by Britain and France on Germany for its invasion of Poland. However, the conflicts leading to this war began perhaps as early as 1936 when Adolf Hitler of Germany ordered his troops into the Rhineland and culminated in March 1938 when Hitler overtook Austria and then six months later demanded the Sudetenland region of Czechoslovakia. These events, and the unknown light in the night sky that announced it, occurred during the reign of Pope Pius XI, just as Our Lady had foretold to Lucia and her cousins back in July 1917.[146]

---

[146] Schulte, Paul C. Archbishop of Indianapolis, Our Lady of Fatima's "Peace Plan From Heaven" January 15, 1950, Page 15. Also, http://www.theholyrosary.org/fatimaapparitions.

1942 - 1952

Pope Pius XII received word of Lucia's interpretation of the strange lights. Lucia had never really believed the lights to be the Northern Lights as was explained at the time and it is reasonable to suspect that she may have conveyed those thoughts to the Pope as well. Regardless, the Pope did consecrate the whole world to the Immaculate Heart of Mary in 1942 with a particular mention of Russia.[147] Privately, Lucia doubted that such a general consecration fulfilled the very specific requirement of Our Lady as expressed in the vision. She demanded the Holy Father's consecration of Russia, commenting, "but it has not been done in the form indicated by Our Lady: I do not know whether Our Lady accepts it, done in this way, as complying with her promises."[148] On January 2, 1944, Our Lady appeared to Sister Lucy yet again following Lucia's anguish at being asked to reduce to writing the Third Secret that was given her by Our Lady in July 1917. In granting permission to write the Third Secret, Our Lady asks it to be revealed to the world not later than 1960.

In a July 15, 1946 interview with Fr. William Thomas Walsh, Lucia made no secret of the fact that "Our Lady did not ask for the consecration of the world to her Immaculate Heart. What she demanded specifically was the consecration of Russia…. What Our Lady wants is that the Pope and all the bishops in the world shall consecrate Russia to Her Immaculate Heart on one special day. If this is done, she will convert Russia and there will be peace. If it is not done, the errors of Russia will spread throughout every country in the world." When asked, if "this means every country, without exception, will be overcome by communism," Lucia responded, "Yes."[149]

---

[147] http://www.theholyrosary.org/fatimaapparitions.
[148] Walsh, William Thomas, Our Lady of Fatima, Image Book, Doubleday Publishing, 1954. pages 222.
[149] Ibid, page 221. Also, http://www.theholyrosary.org/fatimaapparitions.

PART V

FATIMA'S MESSAGE, PROMISES AND SECRETS

THE MESSAGE

In 1917, the world appeared to be on a ruinous course culminated perhaps with the horrors of the very first World War ever experienced by earth's inhabitants. Hundreds of thousands lay dead from the violent fighting, a flu pandemic ravished much of the world and an assault on religion was undertaken by secular political influences that threatened to abolish all religion from the predominantly Catholic Country of Portugal, and perhaps beyond, within two generations.

It is within this backdrop that God chose to send a very special emissary to deliver a message of redemption to the world through three young shepherd children in Fatima, Portugal. "The message was a summons to conversion, faith, prayer, penance and hope."[150] The Mother of God herself appeared with instructions for the children to pray the Rosary every day to obtain peace for the world; to make sacrifices for the conversion of sinners and in reparation for offenses committed against God and Our Lady's Immaculate Heart. She also warned that people must amend their lives and ask pardon for their sins. Subsequent Apparitions called for a special devotion to Mary's Immaculate Heart and the completion of the First Saturday Communions of reparation.

In the year 2000, then Cardinal Joseph Ratzinger, speaking as the prefect of the Congregation for the Doctrine of the Faith, explained that unlike the "public revelation which came to completion in Christ, as enunciated in the New Testament," the "private revelation" of Mary to the children of Fatima has three elements. First, nothing of the message is contrary to faith or morals; second, public disclosure is not illegal; and, third, "the faithful are under no obligation to accept the help offered in the message. Cardinal Ratzinger confirmed his statement after his election as Pope Benedict XVI, the 266th Pope of the Holy Roman Catholic Church.

---

[150] Columbia Magazine, Volume 97, Number 5, published in May 2017 by the Knights of Columbus. Page 19.

The Catholic Church has long held that it is not the role of such "private revelations" to "improve or complete Christ's definitive Revelation, but to help live more fully by it in a certain period of history."[151]

THE PROMISES

As discussed, the Mother of God not only called the three shepherds of Fatima to prayer, sacrifice and devotions to Her Immaculate Heart, but She provided instruction on how to achieve this and gave a promise of what would happen if people of all stripes heeded her call. For example, if you pray the Rosary every day adding at the end of each decade the words, *'Oh my Jesus, forgive us, save us from the fire of hell. Lead all souls to Heaven, especially those who are in most need,'* then world peace will be achieved.

Likewise, if you make many sacrifices, saying with each sacrifice, *"Oh Jesus, it is for love of you, for the conversion of sinners, and in reparation for the sins committed against the Immaculate Heart of Mary,"* that I sacrifice, then God will stop being offended, and thus will recant his promised outbreak of a more terrible war, famine, and persecutions of the Church and of the Holy Father.

Our Lady also promised to *"come to ask for the consecration of Russia to my Immaculate Heart, and the Communion of Reparation on the First Saturdays.* She again promised what would happen if these requests were met with compliance.

> *"If my requests are heeded, Russia will be converted and there will be peace. If not, she will spread her errors throughout the world, causing wars and persecution of the Church. The good will be martyred, the Holy Father will have much to suffer, various nations will be annihilated. In the end, my Immaculate Heart will triumph. The Holy*

---

[151] Ibid, page 20.

*Father will consecrate Russia to me, and she will be con-
verted, and a period of peace will be granted to the world.*

Finally, On December 10, 1925, Our Lady fulfilled this promise. She appeared in a vision to Lucia to ask for the consecration of Russia to Her Immaculate Heart and to provide very explicit instruction of how to achieve this.

*"Look my daughter, at my heart encircled with thorns, with
which ungrateful men wound it every moment by their blasphemies and ingratitude. Give me consolation, you at least;
and announce for me that I promise to assist at the hour of
death, with the graces necessary for salvation, all who on
the first Saturday of five consecutive months confess, receive Holy Communion, recite five decades of the Rosary,
and keep me company for fifteen minutes meditating on the
mysteries of the Rosary, with the purpose of making reparation to me."*

Learning from the Holy Mother of God Herself what we must do on five consecutive Saturdays does not necessarily satisfy the curiosity as to why Our Lady would ask for this devotion. Jesus himself provided those reasons to Lucia in two separate, 1930 revelations, one occurring on the evening of May 29th and the other on the evening of May 30th. Lucia sent this information to Fr. Jose Bernardo Gonzalves in a letter on June 12, 1930.

*"My daughter," the Lord said to Lucia, "the motive is sim-
ple: there are five ways in which people offend me, and blas-
pheme against the Immaculate Heart of Mary.*

1. *The blasphemies against the Immaculate Conception,*
2. *Against Her virginity,*
3. *Against the divine maternity, refusing at the same time
   to accept her as the Mother of all mankind,*

4. *Those who try publicly to implant in the children's hearts,*

    indifference, contempt and even hate against this Immaculate Mother, and

5. *Those who insult her directly in her sacred images.*"[152]

So, there it is! The Mother of Jesus has asked for the completion of five First Saturday devotions to her Immaculate Heart and Jesus has provided the motivation for this requirement. The final piece was provided by Our Lady. That is the detailed instruction for completion of the First Saturdays. Our Lady required that the First Saturdays contain six distinct elements that are relatively self-explanatory. They are:

1. Confessing one's sins to a priest,
2. Receiving Holy Communion in a state of grace,
3. Praying five decades of the Rosary,
4. Meditating for fifteen minutes on one or more of the Mysteries of the Rosary,
5. Doing these things in the spirit of Reparation to the Immaculate Heart of Mary, and,
6. Observing these practices on the First Saturday of five consecutive months.

The Mother of God has made one additional promise regarding this devotion. For those who faithfully and fervently complete the Five First Saturdays devotion to Mary's Immaculate Heart, Our Lady will provide all the graces necessary for that person to attain salvation.

[152] Ahr, Most Rev. George W., Why Five First Saturdays?, The Blue Army of Our Lady of Fatima, Washington, N.J.

THE SECRETS

Included in the delivery of the primary message that Our Lady provided to the children of Fatima were three visions that reinforced that message. Our Lady asked the children to refrain from speaking of these secrets, saying *"Do not tell this to anybody. Francisco, yes, you may tell him."* This is a request that the children took very seriously. Even after being: kidnapped by the government officials; held captive to prevent them from going to the Cova da Iria at the appointed time of the August Apparition; jailed with adult criminals; threatened with death by being slowly lowered into a vat of boiling oil; separated from each other and told that each had been tortured and killed in that way, the children still faithfully honored Our Lady's request of secrecy.

So how is it then that the secrets were revealed? Lucia revealed the first two secrets in her August 1941 Memoir, only with the greatest reluctance, after much prayer, and in total obedience to a direct order of the Bishop. In fact, she was granted permission to do so by Our Lady in an Apparition on December 17, 1927. Yet the third secret, she guarded even more closely. It was in 1943, when Lucia fell seriously ill with influenza and pleurisy, that Bishop Silva of Leiria visited her and suggested she write the third secret down to ensure its survival in the event of her death. At the time Lucia was a nun in the Carmelite Order. "Carmelites obedience requires that orders from superiors be regarded as coming directly from God." This presented a dilemma for Lucia. Which is of greater weight, a direct request of secrecy given by Our Lady or the indirect order from God's representative that the secret be disclosed. As she pondered the quandary, "Bishop Silva sent Lucia a letter containing a direct order to record the secret." On January 3, 1944, following anguished prayer and permission from Our Lady granted in a vision the night prior, Lucia wrote the third secret on a piece of paper and placed it in an envelope that she sealed and secured. On the outside of the envelope, as instructed by Our Lady in Lucia's vision, she wrote that the letter was to be opened and read prior to 1960. In June 1944, that envelope was delivered to Bishop Silva who kept it in his possession until 1957, at which time it was delivered to the Vatican.

The envelope was opened by the Pope in 1960, but the third secret that was contained within it was not made public until Cardinal Angelo Sodano announced on May 13, 2000, that it would be released. A text of the third secret was issued by the Vatican on June 26, 2000.

So, what are these secrets that Our Lady shared with Lucia, Francisco and Jacinta on July 13, 1917? The first two secrets have been described previously as Lucia recounted them for the world to see in her Remembrances. They are:

THE FIRST SECRET
THE VISION OF HELL:

"Sacrifice yourselves for sinners, and say many times, especially whenever you make some sacrifice: Oh Jesus, it is for love of you, for the conversion of sinners, and in reparation for the sins committed against the Immaculate Heart of Mary."

As she spoke these words, Our Lady stretched out her hands, as before, emulating rays of light that seemed to penetrate directly into the earth, exposing to the children a sea of fire. "Plunged in this fire were demons and souls in human form, like transparent embers, all blackened or burnished bronze, floating about in the conflagration, now raised into the air by the flames that issued from within themselves together with great clouds of smoke now falling back on every side like sparks in huge fires, without weight or equilibrium, amid shrieks and groans of pain and despair."

The vision horrified the children and made then tremble with fear causing Lucia to scream. "The demons could be distinguished by their terrifying and repellent likeness to frightful and unknown animals, black and transparent like burning coals. Terrified and as if to plead for succor," the children looked up at the Lady, who so kindly, and ever so sadly, said to them, *"You have seen Hell where the souls of poor sinners go.* [153]

---

[153] Walsh, William Thomas, Our Lady of Fatima, Image Book, Doubleday Publishing, 1954. page 79-80. Also, http://www.theholyrosary.org/fatimaapparitions.

THE SECOND SECRET
INSTRUCTIONS FOR SAVING SOULS FROM HELL
AND RECONVERTING THE WORLD TO CHRISTIANITY

To save them, God wishes to establish in the world devotion to My Immaculate Heart. If what I say to you is done, many souls will be saved and there will be peace. The war is going to end, but if people do not cease offending God, a worse one will break out during the pontificate of Pius XI. When you see the night illumined by an unknown light, know that this is the great sign given you by God that he is about to punish the world for its crimes, by means of war, famine, and persecutions of the Church and of the Holy Father. To prevent this, I shall come to ask for the consecration of Russia to my Immaculate Heart, and the Communion of Reparation on the First Saturdays. If my requests are heeded, Russia will be converted and there will be peace. If not, she will spread her errors throughout the world, causing wars and persecution of the Church. The good will be martyred, the Holy Father will have much to suffer, various nations will be annihilated. In the end, my Immaculate Heart will triumph. The Holy Father will consecrate Russia to me, and she will be converted, and a period of peace will be granted to the world. Do not tell this to anybody. Francisco, yes, you may tell him. When you pray the Rosary, say after each mystery, 'Oh my Jesus, forgive us, save us from the fire of hell. Lead all souls to Heaven, especially those who are in most need.' "[154]

---

[154] Walsh, William Thomas, Our Lady of Fatima, Image Book, Doubleday Publishing, 1954. page 79-80. Also http://www.theholyrosary.org/fatimaapparitions.

THE THIRD SECRET
THE CHRISTIAN PERSECUTION

The text of the letter in which Lucia revealed the third secret is reprinted here in its entirely as released by the Vatican on June 26, 2000.

"The third part of the secret revealed at the Cova da Iria-Fatima, on 13 July 1917.

> I write in obedience to you, my God, who command me to do so through his Excellency the Bishop of Leiria and through your Most Holy Mother and mine.
>
> After the two parts which I have already explained, at the left of Our Lady and a little above, we saw an Angel with a flaming sword in his left hand; flashing, it gave out flames that looked as though they would set the world on fire; but they died out in contact with the splendor that Our Lady radiated towards him from her right hand: pointing to the earth with his right hand, the angel cried out in a loud voice: 'Penance, Penance, Penance!' And we saw in an immense light that is God: 'something similar to how people appear in a mirror when they pass in front of it' a Bishop dressed in White 'we had the impression that it was the Holy Father'. Other Bishops, Priests, men and women Religious going up a steep mountain, at the top of which there was a big Cross of rough-hewn trunks as of a cork-tree with the bark; before reaching there the Holy Father passed through a big city half in ruins and half trembling with halting step, afflicted with pain and sorrow, he prayed for the souls of the corpses he met on his way; having reached the top of the mountain, on his knees at the foot of the big Cross he was killed by a group of soldiers who fired bullets and arrows at him, and in the same way there died one after another the other Bishops, Priests, men and women Religious, and the various lay people of different ranks and positions. Beneath the two arms of the Cross there

were two Angels each with a crystal aspersorium in his hand, in which they gathered up the blood of the Martyrs and with it sprinkled the souls that were making their way to God." Tuy-3-1-1944

PART VI
THE CONTROVERSY

1981

MAY 13

Pope John Paul II, arguably the most charismatic Pope of modern times, stepped into his specially-made, white, open-top Jeep, better known as the Pope-mobile, at about 4:50 in the afternoon of May 13, 1981. He was just about to start his weekly general audience in St. Peter's Square. The Jeep began its slow trek around the elliptical-shaped plaza, stopping periodically to allow Pope John Paul to reach out from the vehicle to shake hands and to pick up and kiss small children, much to the delight of their enthusiastic parents.

At about 5:19 PM, the Pope's vehicle came to a stop just southwest of the Basilica steps. Twenty three-year old Mehmet Ali Agca, a Turkish man with boyish good looks, was among the thousands in the festive crowd, but Agca offered no child for the Pope to kiss, nor did he come to shake hands with the Pontiff. Rather, he reached into his pocket, took a 9mm Browning handgun firmly in his grasp, removed it from his pocket and fired six shots in the direction of John Paul from a distance of only a few yards. Four of those bullets found the intended target. Two bullets hit the Pope in the abdomen, narrowly missing his vital organs, a third hit him in his left arm and the fourth in his left hand. The other two bullets missed the Pope, but did injure two people. Ann Odre, a sixty-year-old American was struck in the chest while a twenty-one-year-old Jamaican woman, Rose hill, was hit in the arm. "John Paul clutched his chest and slumped into the arms of his aids as a bright red stain slowly extended across his white cassock."[155] Agca was immediately grabbed by bystanders who knocked the weapon out of his hand and detained him until the police arrived to arrest him. As he was led away, Agca repeated several times, "I couldn't care less about life. As if to emphasize the point, police found in his

---

[155] "Blitz, Matthew, "The Unsolved Case of the Attempted Assassination of Pope John Paul." September 21, 2015, http://www.atlasobscura.com/articles/the-unsolved-case-of-the-attempted-assassination-of-pope-john-paul-ii.

pocket a note that read, "I, Agca, have killed the Pope so that the world may know of the thousands of victims of imperialism."[156]

The Pope, meanwhile, was taken to Gemelli Hospital in Rome where he would undergo five and a half hours of surgery that saved his life. At least one of the bullets was successfully removed from the Pontiff's abdomen during the surgery.

Agca had killed before. He was jailed in 1979 for the high-profile murder of Abdi Ipekci, a newspaper editor who authored articles exposing far-right groups from Turkey, but escaped from prison by slipping into a prison guard's uniform and walking out. Shortly after his escape, the Turkish paper Milliyet published a letter that Agca had submitted in which he threatened to kill the Pope for being an "agent of Russian and U.S. imperialism."

The ease with which Agca escaped from prison has led to speculation that he was part of a widespread conspiracy but the exact reason why the Pope was targeted remains unclear. What is clear is that Pope John Paul II believed he owed his survival to the direct intervention of the Immaculate Heart of Mary, for his thoughts and many of his actions following the attempt on his life were very much occupied by the events of Fatima.

On May 13, 1982, one year after the assassination attempt in St. Peter's Square and the 65th anniversary of the first apparition of Our Lady to the children, Pope John Paul II travelled to Fatima, where he met Sr. Lucia. The Holy Father visited the various sites associated with the Apparitions. Then, "On the occasion of a visit to Rome by the Bishop of Leiria-Fatima, the Pope decided to give him the bullet which had remained in the jeep after the assassination attempt, so that it might be kept in the shrine. By the Bishop's decision, the bullet was later set in the crown of the statue of Our Lady of Fatima.[157] In December of 1983, Pope John Paul II visited Agca in his jail cell to forgive him for his transgression. He had, in fact, expressed his forgiveness of the would-be assassin shortly after the shooting, but visited Agca to provide the world an example of the type of absolute forgiveness to which we are all called.

---

[156] Ibid.
[157] http://www.theholyrosary.org/fatimaapparitions and the text of the announcement made by Cardinal Angelo Sodano, the Secretary of State, following the Mass presided over by Pope John Paul II at Fatima on May 13, 2000.

In 1984, the grateful Pope requested that the statue of Our Lady from Fatima's Capelinha, the one presented by Gilberto Fernandes dos Santos, from Torres Novas and contained in the "Little Chapel" that was built in 1922 on the site of the holm-oak tree, be sent to Rome where in collegial union with the Bishops of the Church, he specifically consecrated the world to the Immaculate Heart of Mary on March 25, 1984, the feast of the Annunciation. He repeated the consecration on October 8, 2000 after again having requested that the statue be sent to Rome.[158]

In 2000, on the 83rd anniversary of the first Apparition of Our Lady to the three shepherds of Fatima, Pope John Paul II beatified Francisco and Jacinta Marto. The celebration of beatification was attended by more than 700,000 people and the children's cause for canonization was placed under consideration, a cause that would be realized on May 13, 2017 when Pope Francis made the two children saints on the 100th anniversary of the Apparition.

Despite having been sentenced to life in prison just two months after the shooting, the jail cell meeting between Pope John Paul II and Agca in which the Pope offered his forgiveness, and a subsequent clemency granted by the Italian President, provided Agca with his freedom once more. In 2010, Agca was released from his prison cell and made a free man. Pope John Paul II would not live to see Agca's release, however, as the Pontiff died in 2005, but the forgiveness granted by the leader of 1.2 billion Catholics worldwide evidently touched the would-be assassin. In December of 2014, Agca visited the Vatican one more time, but this time, it was not with the intention of making a political statement, but rather to lay flowers at the grave of the Pope he tried to kill some thirty-three years earlier.

---

[158] http://www.theholyrosary.org/fatimaapparitions.

The failed assassination of Pope John Paul II has unwittingly become the source of what is perhaps the only controversy (at least in the hearts of the faithful) regarding the events of Our Lady's appearance over one hundred years ago. The Catholic Church contends that the 1981 attempted assassination is the fulfillment of the third secret revealed to the children by the Mother of God, while some of the faithful believe there has been a Vatican cover-up of future events so horrific that disclosure will create widespread panic and pandemonium.

To understand the source and extent of the controversy, it may prove worthwhile to review the events related to the Third Secret as they unfolded. A chronological sequence has been prepared by a 1978 group known as the Fatima Center, "a grass roots association of Catholic priests and lay people whose mission is," according to its website, "to make known the full Message of Our Lady of Fatima, and promote devotion to the Immaculate Heart of Mary."[159]

Father Nicholas Gruner, the organization's director until he fell victim to a sudden heart attack while working in his Fatima Center office in Ontario on the night of April 29, 2015, dedicated his life to making the Message of Our Lady of Fatima known, understood, appreciated, and obeyed. His insistence that there is an organized Vatican cover-up of the Third Secret has understandably created some distance between his organization and the Church. Church officials have suspended Fr. Gruner from the priesthood. Fr. Gruner contended that his suspension was not done legally and was therefore devoid of merit. To appropriately represent all that Fr. Gruner has claimed without subjective interpretation or bias, the chronology presented by The Fatima Center is reprinted here verbatim.

- **"1917, July 13,** – Our Lady of Fatima gives a secret in three parts to the three shepherd children.

- **1941** – Sister Lucia reveals the first two parts of the Secret in her Memoirs, first on August 31st in her Third Memoir and then again on December 8 in her Fourth Memoir.

---

[159] The Fatima Center, "What is the Fatima Center." 2017. http://www.fatima.org/apostolate/witfc.pdf

- **1943, October** – The Bishop of Fatima gives Sister Lucy a formal, written order to write down the Third Secret. Sister Lucy tries to obey immediately, but for over two months is mysteriously unable to commit the Third Secret to paper.

- **1944, January 2,** – Our Lady appears to Sister Lucy and bids her to write down the Third Secret. Our Lady asks it to be revealed to the world not later than 1960. When later asked why the people had to wait for the Third Secret to be revealed in 1960, Sister Lucy states. "Because the Blessed Virgin wishes it so," and "It [the Third Secret] will be clearer then." The Third Secret is later delivered in person by Sister Lucy to her confessor bishop who in turn delivers it to the Bishop of Fatima, Jose da Silva, on June 17.

- **1944, January 3,** – A photograph of Bishop da Silva posing in front of the 25-line text of the Third Secret, which is enclosed in the bishop's own outer envelope, appears in *Life* magazine.

- **1952, September** – Austrian Jesuit Father Joseph Schweigl, sent by Pope Pius XII to interrogate Sister Lucy about the Third Secret, states that the Secret is in two parts. He later confides to one of his colleagues, "I cannot reveal anything of what I learned at Fatima concerning the Third Secret, but I can say that it has two parts: *one concerns the Pope.* The other, logically – although I must say nothing – would have to be the continuation of the words: *In Portugal, the dogma of the Faith will always be preserved.*"

- **1957, March** – Bishop John Vernancio holds up to a strong light the outer envelope of Bishop da Silva (photographed for *Life* magazine in 1949) containing an inner envelope of Sister Lucy, inside of which he sees the paper upon which is written the Third Secret. He carefully notes that the Secret is *about 25 lines long and is written on a single sheet of paper* with ¾ *centimeter margins* on both sides. On April 16, the Third Secret is received in the Vatican and placed in a safe in the papal apartments.

- **1957, December 26** – In an allusion to the contents of the Third Secret, Sister Lucy tells Fr. Fuentes, Postulator of the Cause for Beatification of Jacinta and Francisco Marto, of many nations disappearing from the face of the earth, about the crisis in the priesthood, and of many souls going to hell as a result of ignoring Our Lady of Fatima's Message.

- **1958, October** – The well-known magazine *Paris-Match* publishes a photo of the wooden safe in Pope Pius XII's apartment in which was kept the Third Secret of Fatima.

- **1959, August 17** – Pope John XXIII reads the 25-line text of the Third Secret which was taken from the papal apartment and then has his personal secretary, Msgr. Loris Capovilla, write on the envelope, "I leave it to others to comment or decide."

- **1960, February 8** – As the world anxiously awaits the full revelation of the Third Secret, the Vatican issues an anonymous press release stating that the Third Secret would not be disclosed and "would probably remain, forever, under absolute seal." Pope John XXIII reads the 62-line text of the Third Secret that same year.

- **1963, June 27** – Pope Paul VI reads the text of the Third Secret kept in the papal apartment after the Substitute Secretary of State telephones Msgr. Capovilla, personal secretary of Pope John XXIII, to inquire as to where to find it. Capovilla testifies to this fact in his certified note of May 17, 1967. It is this text that is later identified by Cardinal Ottaviani as being 25-lines long.

- **1965, March 27** – Pope Paul VI reads the other text of the Third Secret – the one that is 62-lines long. Cardinal Betone claims that Paul VI read the Third Secret for the first time on this date.

- **1967, May 13** – Sister Lucy meets Pope Paul VI in Fatima and asks him to release the Third Secret, but he refuses.

- **1978, October 16** – Pope John Paul II is elected Pope and reads a text of the Third Secret within days of his election, according to a statement to Associated Press in May 2000 by his spokesman, Joaquin Navarro-Valls. The statement by Navarro-Valls is contradicted by Msgr. Bertone when he claimed in June 2000 that the Pope first read the Third Secret on July 18, 1981.

- **1981, July 18** – Pope John Paul II reads the other text of the Third Secret shortly after the assassination attempt on his life in May. According to Cardinal Bertone, the Pope read for the first time the 62-line text of the Third Secret that is kept in the Holy Offices archives.

- **1984, September 10** – Bishop Alberto Cosme do Amaral, the Bishop of Fatima, declares during a question and answer session in the *aulu magna* of the Technical University of Vienna, Austria, "It's [The Third Secret's] content concerns only our faith. To identify the Secret with catastrophic announcements or with a nuclear holocaust is to deform the meaning of the message. The loss of faith of a continent is worse than the annihilation of a nation; and it is true that faith is continually diminishing in Europe."

- **1984, November 11** – *Jesus* magazine publishes an interview with Cardinal Ratzinger. The interview is entitled "Here is Why the Faith is in Crisis," and is published with the Cardinal's explicit permission. Cardinal Ratzinger reveals that he has read the Third Secret and that the Secret refers to "dangers threatening the faith and the life of the Christian and therefore (the life) of the world." Cardinal Ratzinger says in the same interview that the Secret also refers to "the importance of the *Novissimi* [the Last Times]", "the absolute importance of history", and that "the things contained in this 'Third Secret' correspond to what has been announced in Scripture and has been said again and again in many other Marian apparitions, first of all that of Fatima…"

- **1995** – In a personal communication to Professor Baumgartner in Salzburg, Austria, Cardinal Mario Luigi Ciappi – the personal theologian of John Paul II (and of the four popes before him) – reveals that, "In the Third Secret it is foretold, among other things, that the great apostasy [defined as an act of refusing to continue to follow, obey, or recognize a religious faith or the abandonment of a previous loyalty] in the Church will begin at the top."

- **1998** – Howard Dee, former Philippine ambassador to the Vatican, said in an interview with *Inside the Vatican* magazine that "Bishop Ito [the local bishop of Akita, now deceased] was certain Akita was an extension of Fatima, and *Cardinal Ratzinger personally confirmed to me that these two messages, of Fatima and Akita, are essentially the same.*"

   At Akita on October 13, 1973, Our Lady said there would be a worldwide chastisement for sins in which a great part of humanity would be killed and that those who survive would envy the dead.

- **2000, June 26** – At a press conference, Archbishop Bertone publishes the 62-line text which he claims is the entire Third Secret and claims it refers to the 1981 assassination attempt of John Paul II. The 62-line text describes a vision in which the Pope (a "Bishop dressed in White") *is killed* by a band of soldiers. This text, containing *none* of the elements described by Cardinal Ratzinger in his 1984 interview in Jesus magazine, is obviously incomplete.

- **2001, May 16** – Reflecting the growing skepticism of millions of Catholics, Mother Angelica states on her live television show that she does not believe the Vatican has revealed the entirety of the Third Secret. "Mother Angelica Live" as a live program is taken off the air by December.

- **2001, October 25** – Cardinal Ratzinger admits to a "*destabilizing* [of] *the internal equilibrium of the Roman Curia*" due to reports (following the September 11th terrorist attack on New York and the invasion of

Afghanistan) of a recent letter from Sister Lucy to the Pope concerning the Third Secret and dangers to the world and the person of the Pope.

- **2001, November 17** – Archbishop Bertone (later to become Cardinal Bertone, Vatican Secretary of State) travels from Rome to Coimbra to interview Sister Lucy about the Third Secret and claims the interview went on for two hours, but the communique published by Bertone contains *only 44 words* alleged to be from the mouth of Sister Lucy concerning the matters of the Third Secret and the Consecration of Russia controversies.

- **2005, February 13** – Sister Lucy dies at the age of 97 in her convent in Coimbra, Portugal.

- **2006, November 22** – Renowned Italian Catholic commentator and journalist Antonio Socci publishes his book, *The Fourth Secret of Fatima*, which accuses Cardinal Bertone of covering up the complete Third Secret. The book cites the testimony of Archbishop Loris F. Capovilla in July 2006, to Catholic researcher Solideo Paolini, that there are two different texts and two different envelopes pertaining to the Third Secret, that one of the envelopes and its contents – the "Capovilla envelope" – was kept in the papal apartment, not in the archives of the former Holy Office where the text of the version was lodged, and that Paul VI read its contents on June 27, 1963, two years before the Bertone "official account", which claims that Pope Paul VI first read the text of the Third Secret on March 27, 1965. The "Capovilla envelope" and text have never been produced.

- **2007, May 10** – Attempting to discredit Socci, Cardinal Bertone publishes his own book, *The Last Visionary of Fatima*, written in the form of an interview by a Vatican affairs reporter, Giuseppe De Carli, who poses no challenging questions but rather de facto avoids all the issues, including Msgr. Capovilla's explosive testimony. In response, on May 12 Socci proclaims and explains publicly (in his weekly column in the Italian Journal *Libero*) that his own book has been vindicated by the

Cardinal's complete failure to answer it, which Socci calls a disturbing development as it means that there is indeed an ongoing cover-up on the part of the Vatican regarding the Third Secret.

- **2007, May 31** – Cardinal Bertone appears by remote live feed on the very popular Italian TV talk show *Porta a Porta* to again respond to Socci's book. During this telecast Bertone displays not only the text of the version but also two separate, sealed envelopes prepared by Sister Lucy, each bearing the explicit statement in Sister Lucy's own handwriting that "By express order of Our Lady, this envelope can be opened in 1960 only by the Cardinal Patriarch of Lisbon or the Bishop of Leiria."

  The two sealed envelopes, and other revelations by Cardinal Bertone during the telecast, further confirm the existence of two texts comprising the Third Secret in its entirety. Further, the "express order of Our Lady" noted on the envelopes flatly contradicts Cardinal Bertone's earlier repeated representations (only said *after* Sr. Lucy's death in 2005) that Sister Lucy "confessed" to him in private, unrecorded conversations that the Virgin has never given any such order.

- **2007, June 2** – Following the telecast, from which Socci has been excluded, Socci publishes his response in *Libero*. He declares that Bertone has not only failed to "give even one answer" to Socci's book, but "On the contrary, he did more: He offered proof that I am right" and "that as a matter of fact the explosive part of the 'Third Secret of Fatima' exists yet is well hidden..."

- **2007, September 21** – Bertone stages a second television appearance for himself, this time on the Telepace network, to officially launch his own book which had been published in May and also to try yet again to discredit Socci's book for the third time. The press are invited to attend. Socci, as a journalist, appears at the telecast location to question Cardinal Bertone. He acts in a proper way but is forcibly removed from the premises by security guards. During the telecast Bertone once again avoids any discussion of the issues. Instead, he presents a heavily-edited videotape of an interview of Archbishop Capovilla conducted by Giuseppe De Carli, a partisan of Cardinal Bertone, in which the Archbishop not only fails to deny the testimony he gave to Paolini (whose name is never mentioned) about the "Capovilla envelope," but rather fully confirms its existence and location in the papal apartment, and the reading of its contents by Paul VI in 1963, not 1965 as the Bertone "official account" had claimed.

- **2007, September 22** – The Italian newspaper *Il Giornale* reports that before the guards removed Socci from the location of the telecast of September 21, he was able to play for the assembled journalists an audiotape of Capovilla's statements to Paolini during a meeting on June 21, 2007. On the tape Capovilla is heard to state: "Besides the four pages [of the vision of the bishop dressed in white] there was also something else, an attachment, yes." As the reporter from *Il Giornale* concludes, Capovilla's statement "would confirm the thesis of the existence of a second sheet with the interpretation of the Secret" – namely, the words of the Virgin following the "etc."

- **2007, September 23** – Socci again responds to Cardinal Bertone in his column in *Libero*. Socci again calmly demonstrates that Cardinal Bertone is hiding a major part of the Third Secret.

- **2008, January 25** – Christopher A. Ferrara's book, *The Secret Still Hidden*, goes to press; 100,000 copies are printed. In this book, the author gives the history of the Third Secret up to that time. He proves beyond any reasonable doubt that there is a second text, still hidden by the Vatican bureaucrats, which contains the words of Our Lady which follow "In Portugal the dogma of the Faith will always be preserved, etc." He demonstrates his proof using the facts and details provided by both Socci and Bertone. The Italian version of his book is sent to 12,000 Italian priests in June 2008. Cardinal Bertone is sent a copy of Ferrara's book by August 2008 and Bertone acknowledges receipt of the book but refuses to answer the substance of any of Ferrara's arguments.

- **2010, May 4** – Vatican journalist Giuseppe De Carli, co-author with Cardinal Bertone of *The Last Visionary of Fatima* (re-issued in 2010 under the new title, *The Last Secret of Fatima)*, and an apologist for Cardinal Bertone's now discredited explanations of the Third Secret, admits to the *Fatima Challenge* Conference before the TV cameras that "…they could have tricked me."

- **2010, May 11** – Pope Benedict XVI, on his pilgrimage to Portugal in May, stunned the press and the Catholic world by saying that the Third Secret of Fatima tells us that "not only from the outside come the attacks against the Pope and the Church, but the sufferings of the Church come from right inside the Church, from the sin that resides inside the Church…we see this today really in a terrifying way: the greatest persecution against the Church doesn't come from its enemies outside, but starts from the sins within the Church."

- **2010, May 13** – Before 500,000 pilgrims, the Pope proclaimed (in reference to the Third Secret): "Whoever thinks that the prophetic mission of Fatima is concluded deceives himself."

- **2010, July 13** – Giuseppe De Carli dies on the 93rd anniversary of the imparting of the Third Secret by Our Lady of Fatima to the three shepherd children.

- **2011, May 11** – Christopher Ferrara publishes the updated 2nd edition of the Italian version of *The Secret Still Hidden*. Using De Carli's statement from the year before and referring to the 2nd edition of Bertone's book, he further proves that Bertone is still hiding a major part of the Third Secret.

- **2011, July – August** – Christopher Ferrara's book, The Secret Still Hidden, receives an endorsement in the August-September issue of the prestigious *Inside the Vatican* magazine. There the editor Robert Moynihan relates a recent conversation with the late Archbishop Pietro Sambi, who died in July. Archbishop Sambi was Papal Nuncio to the United States and thus a key attaché of the Vatican Secretariat of State under Cardinal Bertone. The report of Moynihan, in part, goes as follows:

> "We [Sambi and Moynihan] were discussing the Third Secret of Fatima, the allegations that the Vatican has not published the entire text of the Third Secret as revealed to Sister Lucia, and the response of Cardinal Tarcisio Bertone, the Vatican Secretary of State, in a book where Bertone states that there is nothing more to be revealed.

> "Archbishop Sambi said, 'Excuse me.' He got up, went out of the room, and came back with a book. 'Here,' he said. 'Do you know this book? You should read it.' It was Christopher Ferrara's The Secret Still Hidden. 'Wait,' I said. 'You are the Pope's representative in the US, and you are urging me to read a book that questions what the Secretary of State wrote?'

> Sambi replied: 'All I am saying is that there are interesting things worth reading in this book. And in the end, we are all after the truth, aren't we? The truth is the important thing…'"

The Fatima Center further notes that the sole surviving visionary herself was silenced by the Vatican when in 1960 it "imposed some very strict conditions of isolation on Sister Lucy, the very same year that the Third Secret was to be revealed to the world…and wasn't." In fact, from that time, and right up until the hour of her death, Sister Lucia was "forbidden to speak about Fatima without direct permission from the Holy See," permission that was never granted.

Prior to the order of silence, however, Sister Lucia spoke to Father Augustine Fuentes. In a conversation took place in 1957, Sister Lucia said,

"The devil is about to wage a decisive battle with the Blessed Virgin, as he knows what it is that offends God the most, and which in a short space of time will gain for him the greatest number of souls. Thus, the devil does everything to overcome souls consecrated to God, because in this way he will succeed in leaving the souls of the faithful abandoned by their leaders, thereby the more easily will he seize them."

Though not able to speak of the Third Secret openly after 1960, Sister Lucia wrote of it in 1969 to one of her priest-nephews, saying, "do not let yourself be deceived." In 1970 Lucia wrote to Mother Martins, a former companion with the Dorothean Sisters, noting:

"It is painful to see such a great disorientation in so many who occupy places of responsibility…the devil has succeeded in infiltrating evil under cover of good, and the blind are beginning to guide others, as the Lord tells us in His Gospel, **and souls are letting themselves be deceived.**"

Clearly, in 1957 Sister Lucia recognized the devil's attempts to wage battle and by 1971 had recognized his early successes. In fact, The Fatima Center notes that many publications, both secular and Catholic, have expressed, not only concern, but skepticism about the Vatican's transparency on this issue. According to Fr. Grunier, even the Washington Post, a secular publication of the United States free press, expressed doubts in a July 1, 2000 edition, about the Catholic Church's official interpretation of the Third Secret. "There is every reason to believe," Grunier contends, "that the Vatican is hiding a text of the Third Secret – the words of Our Lady which would explain how the Pope in the vision comes to be executed by soldiers outside a ruined city filled with corpses – which, when revealed in full, has the power to being about the Triumph of the Immaculate Heart of Mary."

On May 12, 1982, Fr. Gruner explains, Sister Lucia expressed her concerns in a letter to Pope John Paul II, writing,

"The third part of the secret refers to Our Lady's words: If not [Russia] will spread her errors throughout the world, causing wars and persecutions against the Church. The good will be martyred; the Holy Father will have much to suffer; various nations will be annihilated.

The third part of the secret, that you are so anxious to know, is a symbolic revelation, referring to this part of the Message, conditioned by whether we accept or not what the Message itself asks of us: If My requests are heeded, Russia will be converted, and there will be peace; if not she will spread her errors throughout the world, etc.

Since we did not heed this appeal of the Message, we see that it has been fulfilled, Russia has invaded the world with her errors *and if we have not yet seen the complete fulfillment of the final part of this prophecy, we are going towards it with great strides...* If we do not reject the path of sin, hatred, revenge, injustice, violations of the rights of the human person, immorality and violence, etc.

And let us not say that it is God who is punishing us in this way; on the contrary, it is people themselves who are preparing their own punishment. In his kindness God warns us and calls us to the right path, while respecting the freedom he has given us; hence people are responsible."

The Fatima Center notes the importance of Sister Lucia's failure to reference the Pontiff's assassination attempt as the fulfillment of the Third Secret though it had occurred only a year prior. In fact, she specifically writes that "we are going towards it [the fulfillment of the final part of the prophesy] with great strides." The very next day, Pope John Paul was to visit Fatima to consecrate the world to the Immaculate Heart of Mary, yet, it is not the consecration, but rather the annihilation of nations with which Sister Lucia expressed concern.

The Bishop of Fatima, Alberto Cosme do Amaral, addressed a session at the Technical University of Vienna, Austria on September 10, 1984 about the Third Secret of Fatima. His comments were later published in the *Mensagem de Fatima* as follows:

> "The Secret of Fatima speaks neither of atomic bombs, nor nuclear warheads, nor Pershing missiles, nor SS-20s. Its content concerns only our faith. To identify the Secret with catastrophic announcements or with a nuclear holocaust is to deform the meaning of the message. The loss of faith of a continent is worse than the annihilation of a nation; and it is true that faith is continually diminishing in Europe."[160]

Shortly after these remarks were made, the Bishop was pressured to withdraw them, which he compliantly did. However, in 1995, after his retirement, he reaffirmed his Vienna comments in a public interview adding, "Before I asserted in Vienna [in 1984] that the Third Secret concerned only our Faith and the loss of Faith, I had consulted Sister Lucy and first obtained her approval.[161]

Then Cardinal Joseph Ratzinger, head of the Congregation for the Doctrine of the Faith, was interviewed by *Jesus* magazine, a publication of the Pauline Sisters, on November 11, 1984. During the interview, Ratzinger acknowledged that the Third Secret contains "religious prophesy" which cannot be revealed "to prevent [its] being mistaken for a quest for the sensational." Yet, on June 26, 2000, Ratzinger noted that the "Third Secret refers only to events which had already happened (culminating in the attempted assassination of the Pope in 1981) and contains no prophecy concerning the future." He went on to say that "the Third Secret could be the result of Sister Lucy's imagination

---

[160] Frere, Michel de la Sainte Trinite, The Whole Truth About Fatima, Volume III: The Third Secret, Immaculate Heart Publications, Buffalo, New York, 1990. pages 675-676.
[161] Fatima Network, "Published Testimony: (September 10, 1984) The Bishop of Fatima. http://www.fatima.org/thirdsecret/bishfatima.asp.

alone." The dichotomy of those two statements add to the confusion.[162] Cardinal Ratzinger, just two years later, would become Pope Benedict XVI, the 265th leader of the Catholic church.

It is important to note that Fr. Gruner was censured by the Catholic Church for his failure to abide by an order of "his legitimate ecclesiastical superior to undertake some action." Following a warning that "failure to do so would result in his suspension a divinis…he did not undertake the action required of him and subsequently his competent ecclesiastical superior followed through with the threatened censure." Fr. Gruner was ordered, in part, to cease his work and "return to his diocese of incardination" in Avellino, Italy,[163] an order with which he had failed to comply at the time of his death.

Fr. Andrew Apostoli, C.F.R., author of Fatima For Today: The Urgent Marian Message of Hope, disputes those like Fr. Gruner, whose opinion clearly differs from the official view of the Church regarding the interpretation of the Third Secret. In his book, Apostoli addresses the dissenters by listing the objections to two distinct but related controversies: the controversy over the Consecration of Russia to the Immaculate Heart of Mary, and the controversy over the Third Secret. He responds to each objection with an explanation representative of the position of the Catholic Church. The focus here is to the responses related to objections regarding the controversy over the Third Secret. As was the case with Fr. Gruner's timeline, Fr. Apostoli's listing of objections and responses to the objections regarding this controversy is presented here in its entirety:

"Objection: The original Third Secret was written on one sheet of paper.

Many clerics who were familiar with the original text, including bishops who worked with popes John XXIII and Paul VI, said that the Third Secret was written on a single sheet of paper. (e.g., Cardinal Alfredo Ottaviani, who read the Third Secret with Pope John XXIII.)

---

[162] Fatima Network, "Published Testimony: (November 1984) Cardinal Ratzinger. http://www.fatima.org/thirdsecret/ratzinger.asp.
[163] Vere, Peter John, JCL/M (Cannon Law), "Canon Law and Fr. Gruner's Suspension (a divinis): (January 17, 2002) St. Paul, Minnesota, provided courtesy of the Catholic-Culture.org, https://www.catholicculture.org/culture/library/view.cfm?recnum=4086.

The controversy came about when on June 26, 2000, the Vatican released a copy of Sister Lucia's handwritten text in a four-page format. Though there are several possible ways a single sheet of paper can be turned into more than one page (written on both sides, folded and written on multiple sides, etc.) or copied onto more than one page, some critics said that the Vatican copy could not have been made from the authentic text and that some other document exists that contains the real Third Secret.

The Vatican copy of Sister Lucia's handwritten manuscript appears in the document The *Message of Fatima* prepared by the Congregation for the Doctrine of the Faith. In the introduction, the secretary of the Congregation at the time, Archbishop Bertone, stated: 'There is only one manuscript which is here reproduced photostatically,' Sister Lucia herself confirmed the validity of the Vatican text. Archbishop Bertone and Bishop Seraphim de Sousa of Leiria met with Sister Lucia at her Carmelite convent in Coimbra, Portugal, on April 27, 2000. The Archbishop presented two envelopes to Sister Lucia. The first or outer envelope contained the second envelope, which held the Third Secret. Touching it with her fingers, Sister Lucia said, 'This is my letter.' Then, while reading it, she said, 'This is my writing.' When asked if this document was the one and only Third Secret, Sister Lucia answered, 'Yes, this is the Third Secret, and I never wrote any other.'

We have additional proof from Sister Lucia that the photocopy of the Third Secret was authentic. She met again with Archbishop Bertone on November 17, 2001. A communique about that meeting carried this most important point:

With reference to the third part of the secret of Fatima, [Sister Lucia] affirmed that she had attentively read and meditated upon the booklet published by the Congregation for the Doctrine of the Faith [The Message of Fatima] and confirmed everything that was written there. To whoever imagines some part of the secret has been hidden, she replied, 'everything has been published; no secret remains.' To those who speak and write of new revelations, she said: 'There is no truth in this. If I had received new revelations, I would have told no one, but I would have communicated them directly to the Holy Father.'

Objection: The text of the Third Secret released by the Vatican
contains no words attributed to the Blessed Virgin Mary.

The message of the Third Secret was not conveyed in words by our
Lady, but in the various visions the children saw. Our Lady spoke simply by
her actions, as when she prevented the fire from the flaming sword of the angel
from touching the earth and consuming it. Archbishop Bertone explained:

The part of the text where the Virgin speaks in the first person wasn't
censored, for the simple reason that it never existed. The text those people talk
about just doesn't exist. I am not toeing some party line here. I'm basing my
statement on Sister Lucia's own direct confirmation that the Third Secret is
none other than the text that was published in the year 2000.

Objection: The Vatican's copy of the Third Secret contains no information
about a nuclear holocaust, a great apostasy, or the satanic infiltration of the
Catholic Church.

This objection is largely the result of the disappointment that some people
felt when the Third Secret was finally revealed. Cardinal Ratzinger (now Pope Benedict XVI) predicted this disappointment. 'A careful reading of the [Third Secret]',
he wrote, 'will probably prove disappointing or surprising after all the speculation
it has stirred. No great mystery is revealed; nor is the future unveiled.'

The years of waiting for the revelation of the Third Secret combined
with the discretion of the Vatican built up in many people's minds the idea that
the Third Secret predicted some catastrophe, like a nuclear war, a world-wide
natural disaster or a great tribulation within the Church. Some people even developed a 'conspiracy mentality', in which they assumed the faithful were not
being told the truth about what was going to happen in the Church and in the
world. Some critics have accused Vatican officials of publishing a fraudulent
Third Secret or of withholding important information. The problem here is that
no one has ever seen any other Third Secret of Fatima than the one that has
already been released to the public. The burden of proof lies with the critics.
They must produce another document or at least reliable witnesses who have
seen and read it. At this point, none have come forward.

There is one final authority who should be quoted. He is Archbishop
Loris Capovilla, who once served as private secretary to Pope John XXIII. He

had read the Third Secret along with Pope John XXIII and actually held the manuscript in his hands. Certain people have claimed that he had said there were 'two texts' of the Third Secret. However, Archbishop Capovilla made the following clear and definitive statement:

There are not two truths from Fatima, nor is there any fourth secret. The text which I read in 1959 is the same that was distributed by the Vatican…I have had enough of these conspiracy theories. It just isn't true. I read it, I presented it to the Pope and we resealed the envelope.'

As for the doomsday predictions, we know that a terrible worldwide natural catastrophe or a nuclear war could happen, but that would be the result of our sins. This is why we must heed our Lady's message for prayer and penance. We also know that with the spread of secularism and religious indifference, many Catholics are no longer practicing their faith. But again, the remedy for this is prayer, penance and a fervent Christian life, as our Lady requested at Fatima. As for any triumph of Satan over the Church, this is impossible. Jesus himself said so when he told Saint Peter, 'You are Peter, and on this rock I will build my Church, and the gates of Hades shall not prevail against it' (Mt 16:18). It will not be Satan who will conquer, but Jesus with his Immaculate Mother who will crush the head of the serpent.

Objection: The text released by the Vatican is not written in the form of a letter.

Some of the clerics who lived at the time the Third Secret was written mentioned it in terms of a letter, but this was not an emphatic point they were making. The photocopy of the original manuscript released by the Holy See does not have a formal address to the Bishop, however it does have a certain likeness to a letter. The document begins with a title like those in Lucia's memoirs and has a kind of introduction that makes reference to the Bishop:

[title] The third part of the secret revealed at the Cova da Iria-Fatima, on 13 July 1917.
[Introduction] I write in obedience to you, my God, who command me to do so through his Excellency the Bishop of Leiria and through your Most Holy Mother and mine.

Archbishop Bertone said that the point about the document being written in the form of a signed letter is not very important. He said of some of his critics that 'they look at everything through the magnifying glass of their own biases. As a result they latch on to the most unbelievable things.'

As a final plea, let us set aside our doubts and support our Holy Father in the present struggle with our prayers, our fidelity, our service and our love! This would be very pleasing to the Immaculate Heart of Mary! I am absolutely confident that the Holy Father has fully conveyed Our Lady of Fatima's message to us!"[164]

---

[164] Apostoli, Fr. Andrew, C.F.R. Fatima For Today: The Urgent Message of Hope. San Francisco: Ignatius Press, 2010. Pages 263-268.

PART VII
THE MESSAGE OF FATIMA ONE HUNDRED YEARS LATER

World events in 2017 have deteriorated even beyond what they were when Our Lady of the Rosary delivered her message to the three innocent shepherd children of Fatima. In 1917, the countries of the world were involved in a great war, millions were dying, not by war alone, but by the ravages of disease. Organized religion, specifically Christianity and Catholicism, were under assault by various agents of government. People were offending God greatly by turning away from Him and blaspheming His Mother.

Today, various countries of the world are again fighting wars with the prospect for another great war on the horizon that has the potential to claim the lives of millions more than the previous world wars. We are ravaged by diseases both old and new, and people the world over continue to offend God by denying Him and blaspheming His Mother.

Consequently, Russia continues to spread her errors throughout the world as Our Lady foretold and we continue to see an assault on Christianity everywhere, including within the borders of the United States of America. In many countries, Christians are tortured for their beliefs. Richard Wurmbrand, a Romanian pastor writes of the fourteen years he spent in Communist prisons for the crime of "fervent belief in Jesus Christ and his public witness concerning his faith." In Tortured for Christ, Wurmbrand recounts his "years of periodic physical torture, constant suffering from hunger and cold, the anguish of brainwashing and mental cruelty."[165]

His experience is not singular. Hundreds of thousands of Christians are forced to "meet in homes, in basements, and in the woods." Yet, the people of the "underground church" have tenacious faith and remarkable endurance.

Even the United States, with its constitutional right to practice religion without interference from the government, has seen Christianity come under assault over the past three quarters of a century. It begins with subtle changes that appear outrageous, but harmless, to a majority people. Often euphemisms

---

[165] The Voice of the Martyrs, 2017, https://www.persecution.com/public/tfc.aspx?clickfrom=%3d73696465626172.

are used to mask the truth of what is really happening. Murder of innocent children by abortion is called "Choice." The removal of any reference to God or His works in public schools, even those references that are historical in nature, is called "separation of church and state." Death of the elderly due to lack of proper care is called "prudent health care," and the medically assisted suicide of those who are sick or just plain tired of living is referred to as death with "dignity."

But over time, as we have seen, some of these outrageous acts are upheld by the courts and become the law of the land. The following chronology is a small sampling of events that have occurred in the United States over the past 60 years. It graphically demonstrates how desensitized America has become to the erosion of moral values. It is that erosion that tends, over time, to bring this nation and the entire world on a course that virtually no one wants to travel. Each act, however small and innocuous it may seem, may bring the United States and the world one step closer to the retribution promised by Our Lady in her message to the children of Fatima.

- **1958** – Steven Engel, a Jewish New Yorker, joins with other parents to file suit against the State of New York over a state-endorsed prayer that was being recited in schools. The prayer read simply, "Almighty God, we acknowledge our dependence upon Thee, and we beg Thy blessings upon us, our parents, our teachers and our Country."[166]

- **June 25, 1962** – The United States Supreme Court issues a decision siding with Engel and ruling that the required prayer was inconsistent with the Establishment Clause of the First Amendment of the Constitution which reads, "Congress shall make no law respecting an establishment of religion, or prohibiting the free exercise thereof."[167]

---

[166] Matter of Engel v. Vitale, Appellate Division of the Supreme Court of New York, Second Department, 11 A.D.2d 340 (N.Y. App. Div. 1960) https://caset-ext.com/case/matter-of-engel-v-vitale-4.
[167] Engel Et Al. v. Vitale Et Al. Issue: First Amendment – Establishment of religion) other than pertains to parochiaid:) http://supreme-court-cases.in-sidegov.com/l/1875/Engel-Et-Al-v-Vitale-Et-Al

- **1963** – The US Supreme Court banned bible reading and overturned a state law banning the teaching of evolution essentially meaning that the theory of evolution and not the theory of creationism must be taught in public schools.[168]

- **1971** – Norma McCorvey, aka Jane Roe sues Dallas County District Attorney Henry Wade, who enforced a Texas law that prohibited abortion, except to save a woman's life.

- **January 22, 1973** – The US Supreme Court affirms the legality of a woman's right to have an abortion under Section one of the fourteenth amendment to the Constitution which reads, "All persons born or naturalized in the United States, and subject to the jurisdiction thereof, are citizens of the United States and of the State wherein they reside. No State shall make or enforce any law which shall abridge the privileges or immunities of citizens of the United States; nor shall any State deprive any person of life, liberty, or property, without due process of law; nor deny to any person within its jurisdiction the equal protection of the laws." In his majority opinion, Justice Blackmun noted that, for nearly all such references in the Constitution, "use of the word is such that it has application only postnatally. None indicates, with any assurance, that it has any possible prenatal application."[169]

- **1987** – American artist and photographer Andres Serrano submitted his work, entitled Immersion (Piss Christ) to the Southeastern Center of Contemporary Art's (SCCA) "Awards in the Visual Arts" competition.

---

[168] Brown, Matthew, "Supreme Court Ruling 50 Years Ago Set Modern Course For Religion in Public Schools." Deseret News Faith, http://www.deseretnews.com/article/865581712/Supreme-Court-ruling-50-years-ago-set-modern-course-for-religion-in-public-schools.html.

[169] Roe v. Wade Fast Facts, CNN, Updated 8:04 PM ET, Sunday April 23, 2017, http://www.cnn.com/2013/11/04/us/roe-v-wade-fast-facts/, Also Oyez, "Body Politic – The Supreme Court and Abortion Law. Roe v. Wade, https://www.oyez.org/cases/1971/70-18.

The work is a very large photograph of a small plastic crucifix submerged in a glass of the artist's urine. The work was awarded a prize by the SCCA which is sponsored by the National Endowment for the Arts, a US Government Agency. In 1989, the same piece was exhibited in, and favorably received by, the Stux Gallery in New York where the artist received $15,000 for the work, including $5,000 from the government agency. Catholic nun and art critic, Sister Wendy Beckett, stated in a televised interview that she "regarded the work as not blasphemous but a statement on 'this is what we are doing to Christ.'" During a retrospective of Serrano's work at the National Gallery of Victoria (NGV) in 1997, George Pell, the Archbishop of Melbourne, was denied an injunction from the Supreme Court of Victoria that would have prevented the NGV from publicly displaying the work.[170]

- **1996** – Artist Chris Ofili debuted a painting entitled "Holy Virgin Mary" which depicts a black Virgin Mary splattered with elephant dung and laden with pornographic pictures, at an exhibition at the Brooklyn Museum of Art. The Catholic League led a protest of the painting but Fr. George Wilson, a Jesuit ecclesiologist from Cincinnati defends the portrait of Our Blessed Mother surrounded with pictures of vaginas and anuses, spattered with dung and tried "desperately to put critics of the painting on the defensive." Despite the controversial nature of the work, it was sold at Christie's London auction for $4.6 million.[171]

- **2007** – San Diego, California high school math teacher Bradley Johnson was ordered to remove his patriotic and faith-themed banners from

[170] The Guardian, "Andres Serrano's Controversial Piss Christ goes on view in New York." September 28, 2012. https://www.theguardian.com/artanddesign/2012/sep/28/andres-serrano-piss-christ-new-york.
[171] Catholic League for Religious and Civil Rights, January/February 2000. "Brooklyn Museum Debate Rages To The End." http://www.catholicleague.org/brooklyn-museum-debate-rages-to-the-end/.

his classroom after years of display. The banners carried such objectionable slogans as "In God We Trust," "God Bless America," and God Shed His Grace on Thee."[172]

- **August 20, 2008** – The Democrat National Committee refuses to invite the Archbishop of Denver, Charles J. Chaput, to pray or speak at the upcoming Democrat National Convention to be held in Denver. Former Boston Mayor Ray Flynn calls it a "serious oversight" and an "insult" to the values of pro-life Catholics.[173]

- **January 11, 2012** – "The US Supreme Court ruled that the Equal Employment Opportunity Commission had overstepped its bounds in applying secular standards to a minister of religion called to work in a church school."[174]

- **February 2012** – The US Conference of Catholic Bishops declared that the "small alteration" that President Obama announced requiring "all health-care plans in the US to cover sterilizations is "unacceptable" because, among other things, it does not protect the freedom-of-conscience rights of secular for profit employees, or secular non-profit employers, or religious insurers, or self-insured religious employees, or individual Americans." The Act forced Catholic institutions to provide birth control, abortion drugs and other contraceptive services and

---

[172] Theblaze. September 14, 2011. "Court Rules Teacher Must Remove "In God We Trust' Classroom Banners." http://www.theblaze.com/stories/court-rules-teacher-must-remove-in-god-we-trust-classroom-banners

[173] Catholic News Agency. April 3, 2012, "Democratic Conventions Non-invitation of Archbishop Chaput an "insult," Democrat Says." https://www.catholicnewsagency.com/democratic_conventions_noninvitation_of_archbishop_ chaput_an_insult_democrat_says/.

[174] St. Onge, Rev. Charles. Chron.com, "Has Obama Declared War on Christianity?" February 6, 2012.

would require Catholic institutions to abandon their doctrines on reproductive issues or face catastrophic fines forcing them to close hospitals that care for about a sixth of U.S. patients.[175]

- **March 13, 2012** – The "2012 International Narcotics Control Strategy Report" is released to the public and lists 190 nations, each classified by one of three categories: "primary concern;" "of concern;" and "monitored." The Vatican was ranked with Poland, Egypt, Chile and 67 other countries as being "of concern," the middle category. The Obama State Department said the "Vatican made the list because it is considered vulnerable to laundering and because it had recently put a program into place to prevent financial abuses."[176]

- **March 27, 2012** – The US Supreme Court upheld the federal appeals court ruling that prevents teachers from displaying on a classroom wall any statement of religious views such as those displayed by San Diego high school teacher Bradley Johnson. However, a study done that same month concluded that there is a double standard when teaching about religion in public schools. According to the study, the courts are "removing all signs of Judeo-Christianity from public schools. Not only must prayer be prohibited, but a cross and the Ten Commandments must be removed or covered up, a valedictorian is banned from thanking God for his help, a football coach is prohibited from bowing his head during a student-led pre-game prayer, the singing of Christmas carols is banned, and school calendars are required to recognize a "win-

---

[175] PatDollard.com, February 11, 2012, "Obama's War On Christianity Still On: Catholic Church Issues Statement That Obama's 'Compromise Solution' Is An 'Unacceptable' Sham." http://patdollard.com/2012/02/obamas-war-on-religion-still-on-catholic-church-issues-statement-that-obamas-compromise-solution-is-an-unacceptable-sham. Additional Source – Lockhead, Carolyn, The San Francisco Chronicle, "Obama Ignites Firestorm Among Catholics." February 6, 2012.
[176] Theblaze. "Is the Obama Admin Really Attacking the Catholic Church by Placing the Vatican on a Financial Crimes List?" March 13, 2012. http://www.theblaze.com/stories/is-the-obama-admin-really-attacking-the-catholic-church-by-placing-the-vatican-on-a-financial-crimes-list?

ter holiday' instead of a "Christmas holiday." There is also the complete omission of the history of the Founding Fathers' public recognition of Christianity." In fact, the study concluded that Christianity is being targeted while "an analysis of 38 textbooks used in the sixth through twelfth grades in public schools found that since the 1990's, discussions of Islam are taking up more and more pages, while the space devoted to Judaism and Christianity has simultaneously decreased."[177]

- **March 30, 2012** – A Catholic Group was ordered to leave Vanderbilt University after refusing to comply with the University's non-discrimination clause. The non-discrimination clause requires that campus Christian groups (among others) must allow non-believers to serve in leadership roles. One of the larger groups on campus is Vanderbilt Catholic, but at the end of the year, that group will no longer be allowed on campus.[178]

- **April 26, 2017** – A high-school math teacher in Florida banned Christian ninth-grade students from wearing cross necklaces in class. The teacher called Christian crosses "gang symbols" and actually "forced" a ninth-grader to remove her cross telling the young girl the cross was "disrespectful."[179]

---

[177] Townhall.com, "Islamic Indoctrination in Textbooks." April 3, 2012. http://www.townhall.com/columneists/phyllisschlafly/2012/04/03/islamic_indoctrination.
[178] Hallowell, Billy, "Catholic Group to Leave Vanderbilt Campus After Refusing to Comply with Non-Discrimination Policy." TheBlaze, March 30, 2012. http://www.theblaze.com/news/2012/03/30/catholic-group-to-leave-vanderbilt-campus-after-refusing-to-comply-with-non-discrimination-policy/.
[179] Gonzales, Sara, "Florida Teacher Reportedly Banned Students From Wearing Crosses, Now Threatened with Legal Action." TheBlaze, April 22, 2017. http://www.theblaze.com/news/2017/04/22/florida-teacher-reportedly-banned-students-from-wearing-crosses-now-threatened-with-legal-action/.

These few examples demonstrate a gradual but consistent diminution of the moral fiber of the American society and a destruction of the Judeo-Christian principles on which this nation was founded. There is clearly an assault on Christianity generally, and on Catholicism specifically, that has taken hold in this country despite its great constitutional experiment of religious freedom first conceived on this continent by Roger Williams at Rhode Island and Providence Plantations. These examples also provide proof that the assault comes not only from outside the Church, but also from within the faith, as Sister Lucia warned Pope John Paul II.

Ryszard Legutko, who spent forty years in communist-controlled Poland, noted that unlike post-Reformation Europe, religion in the United States was not under the control of the throne because of the separation of church and state. However, he quickly adds, "…until recently, this was widely believed to mean only that there is no [government] established religion. The idea that religion has no access to the public square is a recent phenomenon."[180] It is a fact, Legutko continues, that the "United States was founded on Christian principles and that people who are elected to the public functions are religious people, sometimes with very strong religious views, and that these views affect their political opinion. It's not that religious truth is to be translated literally into policy, but it has a role to play."[181]

Noted author and motivational speaker Dr. John R. Wood, in his book entitled, *Ordinary Lives, Extraordinary Mission: 5 Steps to Winning the War Within*, notes that saints, for the most part, are ordinary people who have done extraordinary things. He explains that there is a saint within each of us and all we need to do is to bring it out. A remarkable concept to say the least, but the three children of Fatima, two of which have already become saints, provide a fine example of how this concept works. They witnessed a miraculous Apparition and changed their lives accordingly. Thousands of others witnessed the same miracle of the sun performed by Our Lady of Fatima. How many of those lives were irrevocably altered as a result and how many resumed their own personal struggle of their daily lives soon after? We witness acts of a miraculous nature nearly every day but we hardly take notice. The birth of a child, the cure

---

[180] Pelowski, Alton, J. "Christian Truth in a Democratic World" Columbus Magazine, Knights of Columbus. July 2017. Page 18.
[181] Ibid

of the stricken, the reformed life of the addicted, the sunrise, the sunset and all that happens in between. Too often the personal struggles involved in earning a living and/or raising a family take precedence over the observance of those daily signs.

John Wood continues,

"These are difficult times for the Catholic Church and the United States of America. There is only one solution to the problems we face...saints! Becoming a saint is a choice, and we must begin choosing the saint within each of us. The biggest crisis of our time is not economic, health care, or vocations, but is an identity crisis. We have forgotten our mission to become saints and forgotten our story as Catholics. We must rediscover that mission and hold each other accountable to accepting responsibility for that mission. Business as usual is not going to cut it. We need heroic Catholicism. We must stop talking, and start walking...stop crying, and start sweating...stop defining ourselves by our sins, and start realizing we are saints in the making! Everything we need to accomplish our mission is in the Church...but the Catholic Church is a sleeping giant. It is time we wake the sleeping giant!

Each passing day brings an instability in the world that drives us closer than ever before to a cataclysmic war between intolerant and quick-to-act nations with fundamental value differences. One recent headline of Sunday July 9, 2017 read, *"Kim Jong-un warns Donald Trump He is Pushing North Korea to the Brink of Nuclear War."*[182] In these dangerous times, who will lead us in the prayers and sacrifices demanded of us by Our Lady of Fatima. If, in fact, the Third Secret of Fatima was fulfilled with the 1981 attempt on the life of Pope John Paul II, it still does not mean the security of our faith. If the Third Secret has yet to come to fulfillment, we must be ever mindful of the consequences of our inactions and of the things Our Lady requires of us if the cataclysmic fulfillment is to be avoided.

---

[182] DailyMail.co.uk, Kim Jong-un warns Donald Trump he is Pushing North Korea to the Brink of Nuclear War. July 9, 2017.

CONCLUSION

Pope John Paul II was "convinced that the contemporary world is engaged in an enormous struggle between the forces of good and evil, between a living faith in the Supreme Being and the absolute rejection of God." He commented shortly after the assassination attempt that the message of "Fatima is more important now than in 1917!"[183]

Pope John Paul II didn't develop that opinion only after the failed attempt on his life. He expressed similar sentiments as a Cardinal in 1978. He was quoted in a November 9, 1978 article in the New York City News as saying:

"We are today before the greatest combat that mankind has ever seen. I do not believe that the Christian community has completely understood it. We are today before the final struggle between the Church and the anti-Church, between the Gospel and the anti-Gospel."

It is perhaps Our Lady's 1917 warning about Communist Russia and the spreading of its errors throughout the world to which the Saintly Pontiff may have been referring in those remarks. Our Lady predicted that "Communism would cause wars and persecutions of the Church, in which the good would be martyred, the Holy Father would have much to suffer and various nations would be annihilated."[184] Some, including Pope John Paul II, believed that these events were characterized by the turbulence of the twentieth century. Others, as we have seen, believe the culmination of Mary's prophecy has yet to be realized.

Regardless of individual beliefs on the fulfillment of Our Lady's Third Secret, it is very evident today that the message of Fatima has not been heeded by the world, not even by all the 1.2 billion Catholics in the world, and that

---

[183] Apostoli, Fr. Andrew, C.F.R. Fatima For Today: The Urgent Message of Hope. San Francisco: Ignatius Press, 2010. page 217
[184] Ibid, page 219.

Russia has not been converted, and that her errors are spreading across the globe reaching even to within the borders of these United States of America.

Fr. Andrew Apostoli, C.F.R., in his book, Fatima for Today: The Urgent Marian Message of Hope, very succinctly provides a list of the errors or sins which Our Lady of Fatima instructed us to reject. They include:

- "The sin of blasphemy against God, our Lady, the angels and saints and those things that are sacred because they are associated with honor and worship of God. Such offenses express an actual, even if indirect, hatred of God." These sins emanate from the atheism that Communism spawns.

- "Sins against life: abortion, euthanasia, embryonic stem cell research, assisted suicide and the whole 'culture of death.' Add to that list murder, physical abuse, gang wars, ethnic and racial cleansing, and all the other violent crimes that come from hatred in our hearts." Fr. Apostoli recognizes the relationship between Communism and the aforementioned culture of death since Communist Russia does "not recognize any God-given dignity to human life. A person was important only to the degree that he was useful to the state. Therefore, Russia became the first Christian nation in the world to permit abortion...Communism teaches the radical equality of the sexes. Women in Russia, and later in Communist China, were required to enter the workforce in service to the state. What was forced upon the peoples taken over by Communism, was unwittingly adopted in western Europe and the United States in the name of equality.... The movement for so-called women's liberation in these countries insisted that women could not take their equal place among men in the workforce unless they had complete control over their ability to reproduce and that control included the power to kill their unborn children.

  As abortion has lessened the dignity of life, euthanasia to eliminate the terminally ill, the handicapped and the elderly has gained acceptance. In an atheistic society, these people's lives are seen to have no value, but only constitute a drain on the state's resources."

- "Another cause of the culture of death, which was fostered by Communism, is the attack on the traditional family…. The family is the building block of society. If families are strong, the society is strong; if they are weak, then the society will be weak…. Karl Marx saw the traditional family as an enemy of freedom and equality…. This notion that the traditional family was the enemy of equality spread to Europe and the United States, where war was declared on those that supported traditional marriage…. Little by little, the legal supports beneath marriage have been stripped away. First divorce was legalized, next cohabiting couples were given legal benefits that once were only granted to married couples…. When marriage is no longer honored and no longer understood as the only proper place for sexual relations, then sexual immorality runs rampant and weakens family life even further. Here we must recall our Lady's words to little Jacinta that more souls are lost by sins of impurity than by any other."[185]

In his book, The Demon in Democracy, Ryszard Legutko notes the various similarities between liberal democracy and communism saying, "…what makes these two systems similar is that both liberal democrats and the communists politicized the entirety of social, individual and communal life. The communists believed the entire social life, even the arts and philosophy, should be permeated by the spirit of communism. The liberal democrats do exactly the same. That is, they believe that everything in the liberal democratic society should be liberal democrat. This aggressive attitude," Legutko points out, "aims to imbue the entire human existence with one set of ideas. In both cases, it implies that you must cut off human heritage and everything that came before in the realm of ideas…. During the last decades, deliberate policies of governments and institutions have also dismantled and redefined the family in order to create a new type of society – a new man. This too, is something that reminds us of the communist regime. To establish a new communist society, the family was the first object of attack."[186]

---

[185] Apostoli, Fr. Andrew C.F.R., Fatima for Today: The Urgent Marian Message of Hope. San Francisco, Ignatius Press, 2010. pages 219-223.
[186] Pelowski, Alton, J. "Christian Truth in a Democratic World" Columbus Magazine, Knights of Columbus. July 2017. Page 18.

Despite the pessimistic tone used in describing the spread of Russia's errors, there is reason for great hope. Our Lady has provided the answer and doing the things she prescribed will cause God to abandon his plans for punishment through the infliction of a great war, the annihilation of nations and the suffering of the Holy Father. Our Lady of Fatima told us very clearly that we must reject sin, say the Rosary every day, make the five First Saturday devotions and sacrifice for the conversion of sinners. In doing these things, Russia will be converted, God will stop being offended and many souls will be saved from the fires of hell.

It doesn't sound too difficult. But what impact can just a few good people with a personal devotion to the Immaculate Hearts of Jesus and Mary have on a world of almost 7.4 billion? God himself provides the answer to that question in Genesis 18:32 in which God promised Abraham that he would abandon his plan to destroy Sodom if just 10 righteous people could be found there. Each of us holds the key to salvation both of the earth and of our immortal soul. It is up to us how we use that key.

Sister Lucia dos Santos died of old age at the Carmelite convent of St. Teresa of Coimbra in central Portugal at 5:25 PM local time on Sunday February 13, 2005. Her death fulfilled the promise of Our Lady to the children in saying that Francisco and Jacinta would go to heaven soon, but Lucia would be here for a long time. Though she was the last of the surviving visionaries of Our Lady of Fatima in 1917, the message of Our Lady as given to Lucia and her cousins lives on throughout the world today as does Her promise of hope.

BIBLIOGRAPHY

Books

Apostoli, Fr. Andrew, C.F.R. Fatima For Today: The Urgent Message of Hope. San Francisco: Ignatius Press, 2010.

Dos Santos, Sr. Lucia, Fatima in Lucia's Own Words. The Remembrances of Sister Lucia, 20th Edition, 2016.

Kelly, Matthew, The Four Signs of a Dynamic Catholic: How Engaging 1% of Catholics Could Change the World: Kentucky, Beacon Publishing, 2012.

King, Greg and Woolmans, Sue. The Assassination of the Archduke: Sarajevo 1914 and the Romance That Changed the World, New York: St. Martin's Press, 2013

McGlynn, Fr. Thomas, O.P. Vision of Fatima. Manchester: Sophia Institute Press, 1948, Reprinted 2017.

Walsh, William Thomas, Our Lady of Fatima. New York: Doubleday, 1947, Image Book, 1954

Wood, Dr. John R., Ordinary Lives Extraordinary Mission: 5 Steps to Winning the War Within, Kentucky: Beacon Publishing, 2012.

Internet Sources

EWTN 100 Years of Fatima. "Message of Fatima." 2017. https://www.ewtn.com/fatima/message.asp

EWTN 100 Years of Fatima. "The Secret of Fatima." 2017. https://www.ewtn.com/fatima/secret-of-fatima.asp

EWTN 100 Years of Fatima. "First and Second Part of the Secret." 2017. https://www.ewtn.com/fatima/first-and-second-part-of-the-secret.asp

EWTN 100 Years of Fatima. "Third Part of the Secret." 2017. https://www.ewtn.com/fatima/third-part-of-the-secret.asp

EWTN 100 Years of Fatima. "Interpretation of the Secret." 2017. https://www.ewtn.com/fatima/interpretation-of-the-secret.asp

EWTN 100 Years of Fatima. "Theological Commentary on the Message." Taken from Romano,

EWTN 100 Years of Fatima. "Children of Fatima." 2017.
https://www.ewtn.com/fatima/children.asp
EWTN 100 Years of Fatima. "Blessed Francisco Marto." 2017.
https://www.ewtn.com/fatima/francisco.asp
EWTN 100 Years of Fatima. "Blessed Jacinta Marto." 2017.
https://www.ewtn.com/fatima/jacinta-marto.asp
EWTN 100 Years of Fatima. "Servant of God Lucia Santos." 2017.
https://www.ewtn.com/fatima/lucia-santos.asp
Society of Saint Pius. "Fatima Apparitions: The Angel of Peace." 2017.
https://sspx.org/en/fatima_angel_apparitions_peace
Botanical. "Holm Oak: Characteristics of a Holm Oak." 2017.
http://www.botanical-online.com/english/holmoak.htm
The Miracle Hunter. "The Messages of Fatima." 2017. http://miracle-
hunter.com/marian_apparitions/messages/fatima_messages.html
The Holy Rosary: Fatima Apparitions. "Apparitions of the Angel."
2017. http://www.theholyrosary.org/fatimaapparitions
Wikipedia. "Fatima, Portugal." 2017. https://en.wikipe-
dia.org/wiki/F%C3%A1tima,_Portugal
Wikipedia. "Assassination of Archduke Franz Ferdinand of Austria."
History Channel. "Archduke Franz Ferdinand Assassinated." 2017.
http://www.history.com/this-day-in-history/archduke-franz-ferdinand-
assassinated
Greenspan, Jesse, History Channel. "The Assassination of Archduke
Franz Ferdinand, 100 Years Ago" June 26, 2014. http://www.his-
tory.com/news/the-assassination-of-archduke-franz-ferdinand-100-
years-ago
Khan, Sal – Kahn Academy. "Gavrilo Princip assassinated Austro-
Hungarian Archduke Franz Ferdinand, setting off World War I." 2017.
https://www.khanacademy.org/humanities/world-history/euro-
hist/world-war-i-tutorial/v/assassination-of-franz-ferdinand-by-gavrilo-
princip
L'Osservatore, June 28, 2000. 2017. https://www.ewtn.com/fatima/the-
ology-and-commentary-on-the-message.asp
Gruner, Fr. Nicholas. "History of the Secret." Fatima Network News.
2017. http://www.fatima.org/f4b/thirdsecret/default.asp
Gruner, Fr. Nicholas. "Third Secret Timeline." Fatima Network News.
2017. http://www.fatima.org/f4b/3rd_secret_timeline.pdf

Gruner, Fr. Nicholas. "Controversy and the Third Secret." Fatima Network News. 2017. http://www.fatima.org/f4b/3rd_secret_trans.pdf

Gruner, Fr. Nicholas. "Sister Lucy Silenced." Fatima Network News. 2017. http://www.fatima.org/f4b/sister_lucy_silenced.pdf

Gruner, Fr. Nicholas. "Cardinal Sodano Reads A Text on the "Third Secret." Fatima Network News. May 13, 2000. http://www.fatima.org/new/newsviews/thirdsecret01.asp

Gruner, Fr. Nicholas. "Third Secret 'Commentary' Raises Concerns Over Whitewash." Fatima Network News. June 21, 2000. http://www.fatima.org/news/newsviews/thirdsecret05.asp

Gruner, Fr. Nicholas. "Third Secret 'Our Plans For Rome in Our Lady's Name…." Fatima Network News. June 27, 2017. http://www.fatima.org/news/newsviews/thirdsecret06.asp

Gruner, Fr. Nicholas. "'The Fatima Crusader' Discloses Vatican Cover-up of Third Secret." Fatima Network News. June 21, 2000. http://www.fatima.org/news/newsviews/thirdsecret08.asp

Gruner, Fr. Nicholas. "The Third Secret Handwritten Text Essential." Fatima Network News. 2017. http://www.fatima.org/news/newsviews/interview.asp

Gruner, Fr. Nicholas. "June 26, 2000 Hoax." Fatima Network News. 2017. http://www.fatima.org/news/newsviews/thirdsecret/hoax.asp

Gruner, Fr. Nicholas. "Reply to the Hoax." Fatima Network News. 2017. http://www.fatima.org/thirdsecret/replyhoax.asp

Gruner, Fr. Nicholas. "Published Testimony: Father Fuentes (1957)." Fatima Network News. 2017. http://www.fatima.org/thirdsecret/frfuentes.asp

Gruner, Fr. Nicholas. "Published Testimony: Nuews Europa (1963)." Fatima Network News. 2017. http://www.fatima.org/thirdsecret/neueseuropa.asp

Gruner, Fr. Nicholas. "Published Testimony: Father Alonso (1975-1981." Fatima Network News. 2017 http://www.fatima.org/thirdsecret/fralonso.asp

Gruner, Fr. Nicholas. "Published Testimony: Pope John Paul II in Fulda, Germany (1980)." Fatima Network News. 2017. http://www.fatima.org/thirdsecret/fulda.asp

Gruner, Fr. Nicholas. "Published Testimony: Sister Lucy's Letter (1982)." Fatima Network News. 2017. http://www.fatima.org/thirdsecret/sisterlucy.asp

Gruner, Fr. Nicholas. "Published Testimony: (September 10, 1984) The Bishop of Fatima." Fatima Network News. 2017. http://www.fatima.org/thirdsecret/bishfatima.asp

Gruner, Fr. Nicholas. "Published Testimony: Cardinal Ratzinger (November 1984)." Fatima Network News. 2017. http://www.fatima.org/thirdsecret/ratzinger.asp

Gruner, Fr. Nicholas. "Published Testimony: (1930s-2003) Some Other Witnesses." Fatima Network News. 2017. http://www.fatima.org/thirdsecret/otherwitness.asp

Gruner, Fr. Nicholas. "Published Testimony: The Seers Kidnapped (August 13-15, 1917)." Fatima Network News. 2017. http://www.fatima.org/thirdsecret/seerkidn.asp

Fatima Network Essentials. 2017. "Historical Context of Portugal (1910-1917) http://www.fatima.org/essentials/facts/histcontext.asp

The Mary Pages, "The Apparitions of Our Lady of Fatima." May 13, 2016, https://www.marypages.com/fatimaEng1.htm

The Miracle Hunter, "Fatima Portugal, 1917." http://miraclehunter.com/marian_apparitions/approved_apparitions/fatima/index.html

Bible Gateway, "The Rich Man and Lazarus." Luke 16:19-31. https://www.biblegateway.com/passage/?search=Luke+16:19-31

Periodicals

Columbia Staff, "Fatima at 100." Columbus Magazine, Knights of Columbus. May 2017. Pages 18-22

Pelowski, Alton J., "Christian Truth in a Democratic World" Columbus Magazine, Knights of Columbus. July 2017. Pages 18-20.

ABOUT THE AUTHOR

Historian Paul F. Caranci is Rhode Island's former Deputy Secretary of State. He dedicated his life to public service, history and writing. The author of seven published books, Caranci's articles have appeared in a plethora of magazines and on-line news services. He has written two award-winning books; Scoundrels: Defining Corruption Through Tales of Political Intrigue in Rhode Island (Dorry Award for Non-Fiction Book of the Year, 2016), and The Hanging and Redemption of John Gordon: The True Story of Rhode Island's Last Execution (Selected by the Providence Journal as one of the top five non-fiction books of the 2013).

Paul serves on the Board of Directors of the Association of Rhode Island Authors (ARIA) and is a co-founder of The Municipal Heritage Group. He is also a former member of the Heritage Harbor Museum Board of Directors, the RI Heritage Hall of Fame Board of Directors, and the Board of Directors of the American Diabetes Association – Rhode Island Affiliate. He served on the Board of Directors of the Diabetes Foundation of Rhode Island for sixteen years serving as its Chairman for two of those years.

Paul is married to his childhood sweetheart, Margie. The couple has two adult children, Heather and Matthew, and four grandsons, Matthew Jr., Jacob, Vincent and Casey. They reside in Rhode Island.

Also by the author...

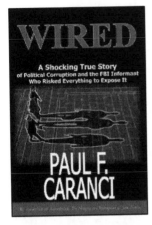 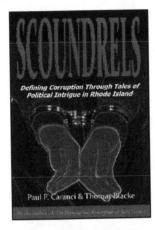 

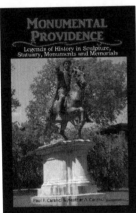 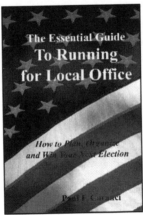 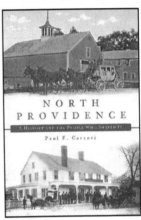

Available at online retailers, bookstores
and www.StillwaterPress.com

Paul Caranci is available to speak at your conference or function,
or to your civic, church, political, or ethnic group or club.
You may contact him at

municipalheritage@gmail.com

www.PaulCaranci.com

62322371R00135

Made in the USA
San Bernardino, CA
17 December 2017